Editor-In-Chief
Amany Saleh

Editor
Krishna Bista

Volume 12/No S1 May 2023

JOURNAL OF INTERDISCIPLINARY STUDIES IN EDUCATION

A Biannual International Referred Journal

Special Issue
*Traveling Concepts in the Classroom:
Experiences in Interdisciplinary Education*

Tessa Diphoorn, Martijn Huysmans,
Susanne C. Knittel,
Brianne McGonigle Leyh, and
Merel van Goch

Utrecht University
The Netherlands

Access this journal online at; http://ojed.org/jise

2023 by *Journal of Interdisciplinary Studies in Education*

All rights reserved. This journal or any portion thereof may not be reproduced or used in any manner whatsoever without the express written permission of the publisher/editor except for the use of brief quotations in a book review or scholarly journal. This journal is a STAR Scholars Network publication and Open Journals in Education.

Published by: STAR Scholars Network

Disclaimer

Facts and opinions published in *this journal* express solely the opinions of the respective authors. Authors are responsible for their citing of sources and the accuracy of their references and bibliographies. The editors cannot be held responsible for any lacks or possible violations of third parties' rights.

STAR Scholars Publications

https://www.ojed.org/index.php/gsm/issue/archive

Journal of Interdisciplinary Studies in Education
http://ojed.org/index.php/jise

Aims & Scope

Journal of Interdisciplinary Studies in Education is aimed at those in the academic world who are dedicated to advancing the field of education through their research. *JISE* provides a range of articles that speak to the major issues in education across all content areas and disciplines. The Journal is peer edited through a blind review process that utilizes a national and international editorial board and peer reviewers. JISE aspires to advance research in the field of education through a collection of quality, relevant, and advanced interdisciplinary articles in the field of education.

JISE (ISSN: *2166-2681)* is published bi-annually by the Center for Excellence in Education at Arkansas State University. The journal publishes interdisciplinary and multidisciplinary theoretical and empirically based-research articles and book reviews related to all aspects of teaching and learning in K-12 and Higher Education. JISE serves as an intellectual platform for the research community. The journal does not have an article submission fee.

The journal is listed/indexed with all major databases.

Among the topics that *Journal* focuses on are:

- Educational leadership and culture of the academy
- Intercultural communication, intercultural relations, student involvement
- Globalization, internationalization, cultural influences
- Internationalization of teaching, learning and research
- Multiculturalism, diversity, and individualism

Published bi-annually, the journal encourages submission of manuscripts by US and international scholars that use quantitative or qualitative methods. Articles combine disciplinary methods with critical insights to investigate major issues shaping national, state, and institutional contexts.

For questions –

Editor-in-Chief: Amany Saleh, Ph.D. E-mail: asaleh@astate.edu

TABLE OF CONTENTS

Articles

1. Traveling Concepts in the Classroom: Experiences in Interdisciplinary Education
   Tessa Diphoorn, Brianne McGonigle Leyh, Susanne C. Knittel, Martijn Huysmans, Merel Van Goch
   1-14

2. The Market for Kidneys: Bridging Introductory Courses in Economics and Ethics
   Martijn Huysmans
   15-28

3. Travelling in the Classroom: Podcasting as an Active-Learning Tool for Interdisciplinarity
   Tessa Diphoorn, Brianne McGonigle Leyh
   29-49

4. How Concepts Travel in Actual Spaces: The Interdisciplinary Classroom as a Behavior Setting
   Annemarie Kalis
   50-66

5. Scholarly Learning of Teacher-Scholars Engaging in Interdisciplinary Education
   Merel van Goch, Christel Lutz
   67-90

Book Reviews

6. The Impoverishment of the American College Student
   Jacob Kelley
   91-94

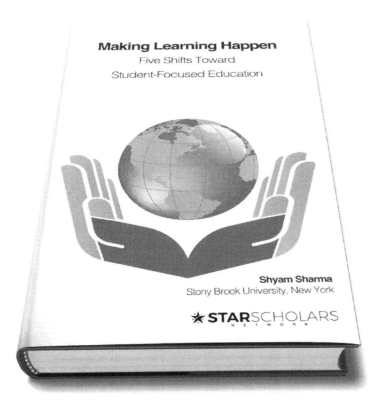

Submit your book proposal at https://www.ojed.org/index.php/gsm/Series

Peer-Reviewed Article

Traveling Concepts in the Classroom: Experiences in Interdisciplinary Education

Tessa Diphoorn, Martijn Huysmans, Susanne C. Knittel,
Brianne McGonigle Leyh, and Merel van Goch
Utrecht University, The Netherlands

ABSTRACT

Interdisciplinary research is widely valued and practiced within higher education. However, there is less attention on interdisciplinary teaching and learning, and existing examples often focus on problem-based approaches. The purpose of this special issue is to explore the potential of a concept-based approach to interdisciplinary education, working with the notion of traveling concepts. Traveling concepts refer to the metaphorical traveling or use of concepts within and between disciplines that impacts their meaning, reach, and operational value. This special issue introduction provides a theoretical and conceptual framework around traveling concepts, which special issue contributions then use to reflect on specific interventions. These reflections highlight the importance of interdisciplinarity beyond a problem-solving frame and provide concrete classroom examples to inspire teachers.

Keywords: Education, Interdisciplinarity, Traveling concepts, reflection

INTRODUCTION

The importance of interdisciplinarity has become a popular refrain in universities around the world. Interdisciplinary research is often regarded as the only sustainable means to solving complex societal problems. Yet much less attention has been given to interdisciplinarity in education and the ways in which interdisciplinary perspectives, skills, and tools can be used for learning purposes (Angerer et al., 2021). In this special issue, we aim to address this gap by reflecting on our experiences of teaching in an interdisciplinary setting.

Our teaching practice is guided by a shared framework and approach: each of us has been inspired by the work of Dutch cultural theorist Mieke Bal in her 2002 book, *Travelling Concepts in the Humanities: A Rough Guide*. Bal argued that a focus on concepts rather than methods provides the most productive approach to interdisciplinary work. Scholars across disciplines have taken on Bal's proposition and have explored how concepts develop and transform as they move within and across disciplines and thus become productive sites of interdisciplinary exchange (Bal, 2002; Bear, 2013; Neumann & Nünning, 2012; van der Tuin & Verhoeff, 2022; Veen & van der Tuin, 2021). Thus, traveling concepts can act as a tool to understanding interdisciplinarity more broadly.

Yet, traveling concepts are primarily explored in relation to interdisciplinary research, while their potential for interdisciplinary education has as of yet been overlooked. We aim to address this gap by showcasing various ways in which the framework of traveling concepts can be used in interdisciplinary education to enable students to develop the necessary skills for interdisciplinary thinking. To translate the notion of traveling concepts into the educational domain, we draw from Allen F. Repko and Rick Szostak's prominent model of interdisciplinarity (Repko & Szostak, 2021) and a four-stage learning model developed at Utrecht University on the basis of Repko and Szostak's approach.

We are all scholars working at Utrecht University in the Netherlands, and are engaged in interdisciplinary research and education. We come from a wide range of disciplines including cultural anthropology, economics, law, literary studies, educational psychology, and philosophy. In our contributions to this special issue, we provide examples and insights from our teaching at different levels (undergraduate and graduate) and in different settings and at different scales (from the seminar to the program level) on how traveling concepts can be used to facilitate new forms of interdisciplinary education. By reflecting on our experiences as teachers, we aim to explore both the pitfalls and promises of using traveling concepts in interdisciplinary education. We hope that by reflecting on our experiences, we can provide novel and helpful insights to our peers working in interdisciplinary education settings.

INTERDISCIPLINARITY IN EDUCATION

For decades, interdisciplinary research has been promoted around the world as a key to solving global challenges (National Academies of Science, 2005; Visholm et al., 2012). Terms such as inter-, multi-, and transdisciplinarity have become buzzwords in academic discourse (Moran, 2010), and there is much discussion on the benefits of knowledge produced outside and between traditional disciplinary boundaries and with new and integrated methods. In the Netherlands, for example, scholars have noted that interdisciplinary research collaborations are "urgently needed," asserting that the complexity of global challenges can only be addressed through "the involvement of many different parties and approaches, new connections and alliances" (De Graaf et al., 2017, p. 38). International and national funding streams and entire university research structures have responded to these calls for greater interdisciplinary research. In tandem with these developments, the theory and practice of interdisciplinarity have become an object of study with an ever-growing number of books, special issues, and conferences dedicated to the topic (e.g., Aldrich, 2014; Angerer et al., 2021; Baptista, 2021; Frodeman et al., 2017; Klein, 1990, 2021). Nevertheless, interdisciplinarity remains an elusive concept, whose definition varies greatly depending on the authors and the context in which they employ it. Moreover, the focus of these publications is largely on interdisciplinarity in research rather than in education. There is a growing body of scholarship on interdisciplinary education (Scholarship of interdisciplinary Teaching and Learning) with its own literature, associations, and conferences (Alexander et al., 2019; Jacob, 2015; Lindvig & Ulriksen, 2019; Millar, 2016; Repko & Szostak, 2021; Rooks & Spelt et al., 2009; Weingart, 2014; Winkler, 2012), but this work focuses either on the theory of interdisciplinary teaching and learning or on prescribing methods and tools. In this special issue, we aim to shift this balance by explicitly focusing on real-life experiences and reflections of scholars engaged in interdisciplinary education.

Interdisciplinary teaching and learning entail two key challenges, which revolve around a particular way of thinking. The first concerns the ability to convey (the benefits of) interdisciplinary research to students, to show that interdisciplinarity is key to addressing complexity and that it entails drawing "insights from relevant disciplines and integrates those insights into a more comprehensive understanding" (Newell, 2001, p. 2). The second concerns teaching students how to engage in interdisciplinary research. This challenge involves interdisciplinary methodology and approaches on the one hand and specific competencies, skills, and attitudes on the other. Here it is important to note that a distinction should be made between education in which interdisciplinarity is the *goal* (e.g., to teach students interdisciplinary research competencies), or the *means* towards a goal (e.g., to analyze complex societal challenges), and between interdisciplinary education and education on interdisciplinary research. The contributions to this special issue address both challenges in various ways. Some focus more on the experience of teaching in an interdisciplinary setting, while others outline the practicalities of teaching certain skills and approaches to foster interdisciplinary thinking.

More specifically, we aim to provide self-reflexive accounts of our experiences in working with concepts in interdisciplinary education. Interdisciplinarity in the classroom tends to depart from a problem-based approach, where students and educators are encouraged to combine methods and approaches from various disciplines to tackle a concrete and predefined societal or scientific problem in search of a solution. For example, at our university, there are a number of excellent problem or challenge-based interdisciplinary educational initiatives for students, including the Da Vinci Project, the TIC to TIC program, and the Inter-University Sustainability Challenge. Such initiatives are worthwhile and productive, yet they also face several limitations. Very often, problems are not well defined, the questions posed are not themselves critically discussed, and those involved find it difficult to find a common language to solve the identified problem. It is hard, if not impossible, to find a common language if those involved do not have a full understanding of the assumptions underpinning different disciplinary perspectives.

As highlighted in the extensive work on interdisciplinarity, there are significant differences between disciplines in how they construct and approach their objects of study, work with theory and methodology, and conduct their research more generally—all of which crucially inform teaching practices (Klein, 1996; Repko & Szostak, 2021). Approaches, theories, and concepts are not only imbued with, and shaped by, scientific, historical, linguistic, cultural, and geographic traditions, they also come with ideological freight and often unconscious biases. Such disciplinary approaches and traditions, as well as the unacknowledged assumptions that come with them, often make it difficult to have productive interdisciplinary conversations, especially in the classroom. To address these challenges, we need to know: What tools and skills do teachers and students need to reflect on these assumptions and biases in the classroom? Which processes and elements are crucial to providing space for the identification and development of a common language? Existing research has identified certain competencies for enhancing interdisciplinary collaboration, but the learning processes associated with these are unclear (Culhane et al., 2018; Parker, 2010).

We contend that a productive framework for conducting such self-reflexive interdisciplinary conversations is to focus on concepts and the way they travel between different disciplines. This approach is inspired by Mieke Bal's *Travelling Concepts in the Humanities: A Rough Guide* (2002), which takes concepts as "tools of intersubjectivity" (p. 22) that allow teachers and students to find common ground as they speak across disciplines. In other words, we propose traveling concepts as a useful addition to the repertoire of "interdisciplinary habits of mind" (Newell & Luckie, 2019, p. 6).

TRAVELING CONCEPTS

In *Travelling Concepts in the Humanities*, Bal proposed a focus on concepts rather than methods as the most productive approach to the problem of interdisciplinarity. Concepts are not merely descriptive; they are theoretical tools or "miniature theories" (Bal, 2002, p. 22) that have been developed and used in different disciplinary contexts to name and define themes, problems, and relevant questions. By giving a name to abstract ideas or phenomena, concepts allow people to communicate and to talk about their experiences and the world, facilitating discussion "on the basis of a common language" (Bal, 2002, p. 22) Concepts such as 'memory,' 'identity,' 'truth,' or 'nature,' for example, are never merely neutral or self-evident, but rather are performative, programmatic, and normative (Bal, 2002, p. 28). This is particularly evident when it comes to controversial or hotly debated concepts in society, such as 'gender,' 'race,' 'equality,' or 'justice.' The fact that they are hotly debated testifies to the power of concepts to shape social life.

In addition to this shaping power, concepts also have the capacity to metaphorically travel between and beyond disciplines, academic communities and cultures, differing in meaning, reach and operational value, sometimes even transforming disciplinary boundaries. Concepts are thus not fixed or static entities. As such, they can facilitate interdisciplinary discussion and innovation "not because they mean the same thing for everyone, but because they don't" (Bal, 2002, p. 11). The differences should not be seen as an impediment to interdisciplinarity but as a catalyst and a necessary precondition. It is through their ongoing travels that concepts become richer and invested with new meanings. Concepts are not simply given, but they are made – *conceived* - and historically situated.

The meaning of a particular concept, therefore, emerges from practice: from the ways it is used, "appropriated, translated and kept up to date over and over again and always with a difference" (Neumann & Nünning, 2012, p. 4). Its power "resides in the scholarly activities it propels, i.e. in traveling processes, rather than in what it is 'in itself'" (Neumann & Nünning, 2012, p. 4). A focus on traveling concepts thus places the emphasis on making explicit the underlying and unquestioned assumptions contained in the concepts we use to describe the problems we face. This, we argue, is a crucial step for interdisciplinarity to succeed. As Bal wrote, because concepts "are key to intersubjective understanding, more than anything they need to be explicit, clear, and defined"(Bal, 2002, p. 22). Only then can they "help to articulate an understanding [...], enable a discussion on the basis of common terms"(Bal, 2002, p. 23).

Traveling concepts have become an important point of reference for interdisciplinary research within the humanities. Through the notion of traveling concepts, we have gained insight into how different disciplines construct, assess, and disseminate knowledge in different ways. Yet it is not only important to focus on the *concepts*, but also on the conception of *traveling* itself. There are various metaphors for the movement of concepts between cultures, discourses, and disciplines that are employed in different contexts, each with its own set of implicit and explicit assumptions and connotations.

Transplantation, for example, which has been theorized in the context of comparative legal studies (cf. Baer, 2012; Berkowitz et al., 2003), describes how a given concept is taken and incorporated into a new discipline, sub-field, or other context. As in the case of organ transplantation, the concept can either be accepted or rejected, depending on the intrinsic compatibility between the 'donor' and the 'recipient.' Clearly, however, while this metaphor may be fitting in certain contexts, it does not cover the full range of possible ways in which concepts move. Furthermore, the metaphor of transplantation presupposes distinct bodies and is too dependent on a rigid separation of the disciplines, whereas the basic principle underlying our approach to the movement of concepts is that disciplines are not islands or discrete bodies, but fundamentally entangled and connected.

Other metaphors for how concepts move between disciplines and discourses are less intentionalist and describe more gradual, decentralized, and dispersed processes. Migration, for example, refers to the way concepts gradually 'settle' and take hold in a new place (cf. Baer, 2012). Like the migration of populations, migrating concepts often encounter formal and institutional resistance and barriers. This metaphor also has its limits, however, not only because it can be difficult to track where specific concepts came from, but also because it can be made to imply that certain concepts are authentically or organically 'native,' while others are foreign, whereas in fact migration – both of human populations and of discourses and concepts – is the default state. Diffusion is yet another way that concepts travel and spread. Bal noted, for example, how at certain moments, particular concepts seem to take on a life of their own and come to proliferate, cropping up in all sorts of appropriate and inappropriate contexts. This, she writes, can result in a dilution of the concept that strips it of its "conceptualizing force" (Bal, 2002, p. 33). Bal here pointed to an inherent risk in interdisciplinarity, namely that through careless application the concepts may become hollow and superficial. In other words, it is not always clear that traveling is a good thing, particularly when beyond disciplinary boundaries (cf. Baer, 2013).

By focusing both on the concepts themselves and different modalities of movement within and between disciplines, the framework of traveling concepts can become crucial in understanding the promises and barriers to interdisciplinarity. Yet, while the potential of traveling concepts for interdisciplinary research has been much discussed, the question of how traveling concepts can be made productive for teaching has so far not been explored. If we contend that concepts are tools and "partners in thinking and making" (van der Tuin & Verhoeff, 2022, p. 6), then we also need to understand how they act as tools in the classroom. It is important to uncover whether and how traveling concepts are bolstering or thwarting understandings and learning processes and whether the framework provides a means for students to identify, explore, and develop interdisciplinary ways of thinking.

TRANSLATING TRAVELING CONCEPTS INTO TEACHING

In order to translate the framework of traveling concepts into the field of interdisciplinary education, we draw inspiration from our colleagues from the Interdisciplinary Education team at our university, who employ a four-stage learning model for stimulating interdisciplinary thinking and for learning interdisciplinary skills. This model draws on existing theories on interdisciplinary and cognitive development by Alan Repko and William Perry and acts as a foundation from which interdisciplinary courses and learning activities can be designed.

The first phase in this model is *disciplinary grounding*. In order to engage in interdisciplinary work, one must first have a comprehensive understanding of the various disciplines involved: their key concepts, approaches, and theories; their epistemology (how knowledge is constructed within a particular discipline); how theories and ideas are validated (which methods are used); and how ideas and insights are communicated. With regards to traveling concepts, this phase entails realizing that a particular word functions as a concept and becoming aware of the work it does or is being made to do, its "travel history" and "baggage" (cf. Veen & van der Tuin, 2021, p. 146).

The second phase is *perspective-taking*. This phase entails analyzing a specific problem or issue from the perspective of each discipline. At this stage, the approach remains multidisciplinary rather than interdisciplinary: the disciplinary insights are considered in parallel as different perspectives, but not yet integrated. For perspective-taking to work, it is crucial that participants see the merit of other approaches and ideas and are willing to identify and reflect on their own prejudice, assumptions, and expectations. For many of these processes, an open mind and willingness to embrace difference are essential.

Once perspective-taking has occurred, space emerges for the identification of commonalities and initiating the third phase, namely *finding common ground*. Combined, the phases of perspective taking and finding common ground entail a self-reflexive process of making one's own use of and disciplinary assumptions about a concept explicit. This process requires situating oneself in a particular disciplinary tradition or community, as part of a particular 'we' who use a concept in a particular way and to mean a certain thing. Furthermore, this means acknowledging that one's own definition of a concept is not the only one and that in other contexts, a different definition may be more fitting and productive.

As noted above, a key challenge and advantage of interdisciplinary thinking is the development of a common language. At this point, when such a common language can be found, one can speak across and through different disciplines about a particular topic or problem. Hence, identifying and discussing traveling concepts can be particularly fruitful at this stage. Finding common ground is thus very often a creative process that entails constant modification, redesign, and reflection.

The fourth phase is *integration*: this phase entails fusing the different perspectives together and creating an innovative and different comprehension or approach. This new understanding is one that could not have been arrived at from one single disciplinary perspective, but that draws on and inherently requires the various disciplinary perspectives involved. This last step is also often a creative process and results in novel models, theories, or methods. This process is then, ideally, applied to a particular topic or problem. Integration cannot occur through one discipline alone. Repko and Szostak (2021) highlighted that integration often demands outside-the-box thinking. For some scholars, integration occurs through dialogue and interactions across two or more disciplines, while others, referred to as integrationist interdisciplinarians, argued that integration "should be the *goal* of interdisciplinary work because integration addresses the challenge of complexity" (Repko & Szostak, 2021, p. 20; emphasis in original).

This four-stage learning model can be applied in numerous ways in and across courses, modules, and entire education programs. Not all four steps will receive equal weight in all cases. In some cases, perspective-taking may be the learning goal, while in others, integration is the ultimate learning goal. This, like all education, depends on what the expected learning outcomes are. In this special issue, we bring this four-step model of interdisciplinary education into conversation with Bal's notion of traveling concepts. We aim to provide pedagogical tools and approaches by which students (and teachers) can understand the meaning, shaping, and making of a concept, as well as its traveling. In the various contributions to this issue, we show how we have done this at different scales and within different educational settings and contexts.

TAKING OFF: PILOTS IN INTERDISCIPLINARY EDUCATION

This special issue consists of a number of case studies that are based on our own teaching practice and experiences. This contrasts with the more top-down approach that is commonly found in interdisciplinary education (e.g., de Greef et al., 2017; Newell, 1994). Each contribution explores ways in which we, as scholars, have experimented with developing, designing, and testing different learning activities at various levels of education.

Most of us are not scholars of education, and our experiences in interdisciplinary education forced us to step outside our comfort zones. With a pioneering spirit, we traveled across disciplinary divides. We are all deeply committed to interdisciplinary work, and most of us practice this in our research as well as in our teaching. Based at Utrecht University, we have formed a close collaboration within the framework of the Young Academy (YA), a platform for interdisciplinary research and education, as well as societal engagement and university policy. We all came together due to our interest in and experience in various interdisciplinary projects in teaching and research. At the outset, we shared ideas on interdisciplinarity and discussed various tools and means to understand interdisciplinarity, such as threshold concepts (Meyer & Land, 2005; Zepke, 2013), boundary crossing (Akkerman & Bakker, 2011), and, of course, traveling concepts (Bal, 2002), which quickly emerged as one of the most productive frameworks for these interdisciplinary conversations. During these interactive sessions, we realized that many of us were engaged in experimenting with interdisciplinary education in various settings. This realization was the point of departure for a more sustained collaboration over the course of four years.

This special issue presents our reflections on that process and on our experiences in the classroom. We reflect on how our interdisciplinary interventions and the notion of traveling concepts allowed us and our students to develop interdisciplinary skills and knowledge. We primarily draw from our first-hand experiences to outline both the promises and pitfalls of interdisciplinarity (see Ashby & Exter 2019; Lattuca et al., 2004; Rooks & Winkler, 2012). Our aim here is not to provide a guidebook on how to practice interdisciplinary education (as, for example, provided by Kelly et al. (2019) in the context of interdisciplinary research). Rather, we aim to share real-life experiences on the difficulties, challenges, and enjoyments of creating an interdisciplinary classroom setting. Our hope is that our reflections can inspire and assist others who are working in interdisciplinary education. We also include the experiences and perspectives of students (Baker & Pollard, 2020), drawing on various sources such as surveys, reflection reports, course evaluations, and informal feedback.

The contributions in this special issue chronicle our experiences with the notion of traveling concepts in a range of different educational contexts and scenarios: undergraduate and graduate courses, in regular education and in honors education, in individual class activities or lectures, in the design and teaching of a course, or an entire minor program. The special issue consists of three core articles, each describing a particular case-study, followed by a reflective conclusion that brings together the contributions, both in terms of the content of the intervention, as well as the experiences of the scholars engaged in the activities. Through reflection and critical analysis, we offer an honest account of the promises and pitfalls of interdisciplinary teaching and learning and provide recommendations for educators interested in working with traveling concepts in interdisciplinary teaching.

The contributions are ordered according to the size of the intervention. In the first contribution, "The Market for Kidneys: Bridging Introductory Courses in Economics and Ethics," economist Martijn Huysmans describes an intervention in a course in the interdisciplinary undergraduate program in Philosophy, Politics, and Economics (PPE). He finds that a short knowledge clip on the traveling concepts of *voluntariness* and *value* can help students build more general interdisciplinary skills. In the second article, "Travelling in the Classroom: Podcasting as a Learning Tool for Interdisciplinarity," cultural anthropologist Tessa Diphoorn and legal scholar Brianne McGonigle Leyh reflect on the making of their podcast series *Travelling Concepts on Air* and discuss how they have been using episodes from this series in their teaching. They show how podcasting can function as a useful tool in education more broadly, but especially for understanding and practicing interdisciplinarity as a form of active learning. Thereafter, philosopher Annemarie Kalis analyzes the interdisciplinary classroom as a behavioral setting in "How Concepts Travel while Students Eat Pizza." She shows the importance of informal exchanges among students in an interdisciplinary honors program bridging philosophy and physics.

Finally, in the concluding article "Scholarly Learning of Teacher-Scholars Experimenting with Interdisciplinary Education," educational scholar Merel van Goch presents a reflection on the contributions in this special issue, drawing on interviews she conducted with the authors. Bringing the different experiences, approaches, and reflections together, she discusses what scholars can learn from engaging in interdisciplinary education, academically as well as personally.

With this special issue as a whole, we hoped to emphasize that interdisciplinarity in education is always an ongoing process requiring continuous practice (Klein, 1990), both for the student and the educator, and never a final state with a final destination. Continuing the analogy of traveling, the notion of travel has very different connotations depending on who is traveling and whether the journey is made for leisure and self-actualization or out of necessity, whether the journey is undertaken willingly or reluctantly, and so on. As literary scholars Birgit Neumann and Ansgar Nünning (2012) wrote, "[v]ariations in scale and scope, the multidirectionality of travels, flows and exchange processes as well as the exercise of power are often overlooked" (p. 6). Yet, they continued, it is precisely *because* of the association of mobility and travel with a certain history of classed and gendered privilege that a critical reflection on modalities of travel may serve to remind us of the fact that "concepts are never neutral or uncontaminated" (Neumann and Nünning, 2012, p. 6) . This statement is important to keep in mind when conducting interdisciplinary research, but it is even more important when it comes to interdisciplinary teaching.

REFERENCES

Akkerman, S.F., & Bakker. A. (2011). Boundary crossing and boundary objects. *Review of Educational Research, 81*(2), 132–169. https://doi.org/10.3102/0034654311404435

Aldrich, J. (2014) *Interdisciplinarity: Its role in a discipline-based academy*.Oxford University Press.

Angerer, E., Brincker, L., Rowan, E., Scager, K., & Wiegant F. (2021). *Interdisciplinary Orientation. Learning to navigate beyond your discipline.* Utrecht University.

Ashby, I. & Exter, M. (2019) Designing for interdisciplinarity in higher education; Considerations for instructional designers. *TechTrends*, 63, 202–208. https://doi.org/10.1007/s11528-018-0352-z

Baer, S. (2013). Traveling concepts: Substantive equality on the road. *Tulsa Law Review, 46*, 59–80. https://digitalcommons.law.utulsa.edu/tlr/vol46/iss1/9

Baker, M., & Pollard J. (2020). Collaborative team-teaching to promote interdisciplinary learning in the undergraduate classroom: A qualitative study of student experiences. *College Teaching, 9*(2), 330–354. https://link.gale.com/apps/doc/A662496410/AONE?u=anon~769c964&sid=googleScholar&xid=1f7a7cf9

Bal, M. (2002). *Travelling concepts in the humanities: A rough guide.* University of Toronto Press.

Baptista, B. V. (2021). Reconfiguring interdisciplinary and transdisciplinary spaces for Arts, Humanities and Social Sciences integration. *Revista EducaOnline*, 15(2), 45–65.

Berkowitz, D., Pistor, K., & Richard, J. (2003). The transplant effect. *American Journal of Comparative Law, 51*(1), 163–203. https://doi.org/10.2307/3649143

Culhane, J., Niewolny, K., Clark, S. & Misyak, S. (2018). Exploring the intersections of interdisciplinary teaching, experiential learning, and community engagement: A case study of service learning in practice. *International Journal of Teaching and Learning in Higher Education, 30*(3), 412–422. https://eric.ed.gov/?id=EJ1199419

De Graaf, B. A., Rinnooy Kan, A., & Molenaar, H. (2017). *The Dutch National research agenda in perspective: A reflection on research and science policy in practice*. Amsterdam University Press.

de Greef, L., Post, G. Vink, C., & Wenting, L. (2017). *Designing interdisciplinary education: A practical handbook for university teachers*. Amsterdam University Press.

Frodeman, R., Klein, J. T., & Pacheco, R. C. D. S. (Eds.). (2017). *The Oxford handbook of interdisciplinarity*. Oxford University Press.

Jacob, J.W. (2015) Interdisciplinary trends in higher education. *Palgrave Communications* 1(1),1 – 5. https://doi.org/10.1057/palcomms.2015.1

Kelly, R., Mackay, M., Nash, K.L. Cvitanovic, C., Allison, E.H., Armitage, D., Bonn, A., Cooke, S.J., Frusher, S., Fulton, E.A., Halpern, B.S., Lopes, P.F.M., Milner-Gulland, E.J., Peck, M.A., Pecl, G.T., Stephenson, R.L., Werner, F. (2019). Ten tips for developing interdisciplinary socio-ecological researchers. *Socio-Ecological Practice Research,1*(2), 149–161. https://doi.org/10.1007/s42532-019-00018-2.

Klein, J. T. (1990). *Interdisciplinarity: History, theory, and practice*. Wayne State University Press.

Klein, J. T. (2021). *Beyond interdisciplinarity: Boundary work, communication, and collaboration*. Oxford University Press.

Lindvig, K., & Ulriksen, L. (2019). Different, difficult, and local: A review of interdisciplinary teaching activities. *The Review of Higher Education*, 43(2), 697–725. http://doi.org/10.1353/rhe.2019.0115

Millar, V. (2016) Interdisciplinary curriculum reform in the changing university. *Teaching in Higher Education*, 21(4): 471–483. https://doi.org/10.1080/13562517.2016.1155549

Menken, S. and Keestra, M. (Eds). (2016). *An Introduction to interdisciplinary research: Theory and practice*(3rd edition). Amsterdam University Press.

Meyer, J. H., & Land, R. (2005). Threshold concepts and troublesome knowledge (2): Epistemological considerations and a conceptual framework for teaching and learning. *Higher Education*, 49(3), 373–388. https://doi.org/10.1007/s10734-004-6779-5

National Academies of Science (2005). *Facilitating interdisciplinary research*. The National Academies Press.

Neumann, B. & Nünning A. (2012). Travelling concepts as a model for the study of culture. In Neumann, B. & Nünning, A. (Eds.), *Travelling concepts for the study of culture* (pp.1-21). De Gruyter.

Newell, W. H. (2001). A theory of interdisciplinary studies. *Issues in Integrative Studies*, 19(1), 1–25. http://hdl.handle.net/10323/4378

Newell, W. H. (1994). Designing interdisciplinary courses. *New directions for teaching and learning, 1994*(58), 35–51. https://doi.org/10.1002/tl.37219945804

Newell, W. H., & Luckie, D. B. (2019). Pedagogy for interdisciplinary habits of mind. *Journal of Interdisciplinary Studies in Education*, 8(1), 6–20. https://doi.org/10.32674/jise.v8i1.584

Parker, J. E. (2010). Competencies for interdisciplinarity in higher education. *International Journal of Sustainability in Higher Education*, 11(4), 325–338. https://doi.org/10.1108/14676371011077559

Repko, A.F. & Szostak, R. (2021). *Interdisciplinary research: Process and theory* (4th edition). Sage.

Rooks, D. & Winkler, C. (2012). Learning interdisciplinarity: service learning and the promise of interdisciplinary teaching. *Teaching Sociology*, 40(1), 2–20. https://doi.org/10.2307/41503319

Roy, S. G., de Souza, S. P., McGreavy, B., Druschke, C. G., Hart, D. D., & Gardner, K. (2020). Evaluating core competencies and learning outcomes for training the next generation of sustainability researchers. *Sustainability Science*, *15*(2), 619–631. https://doi.org/10.1007/s11625-019-00707-7

Spelt, E. J. H., Biemans, H. J. A., Tobi, H., Luning, P. A., & Mulder, M. (2009). Teaching and learning in interdisciplinary higher education: A systematic review. *Educational Psychology Review*, *21*(4), 365–378. https://doi.org/10.1007/s10648-009-9113-z

Van der Tuin, I. & Verhoeff, N. (2022) *Critical concepts for the creative humanities*. Rowman & Littlefield.

Veen, M. & Van der Tuin, Iris (2021). When I say... travelling concepts. *Medical Education*, 55(2), 146 – 147. https://doi.org/10.1111/medu.14400

Visholm, A., Grosen, L., Nom, M.T., & Jensen, R. L. (2012). *Interdisciplinary research is key to solving society's problems*. Danish Energy Agency. https://dea.nu/i-farver/publikationer/interdisciplinary-research-is-key-to-solving-society-s-problems/

Weingart, P., & Padberg, B. (2014). *University experiments in interdisciplinarity. Obstacles and opportunities.* Bielefeld.

Zepke, N. (2013). Threshold concepts and student engagement: Revisiting pedagogical content knowledge. *Active Learning in Higher Education*, 14(2), 97–107. https://doi.org/10.1177/1469787413481127

TESSA DIPHOORN, PhD, is an Associate Professor at the Department of Cultural Anthropology, Utrecht University, the Netherlands. Her research and teaching focuses on policing, security, and everyday authority. Email: t.g.diphoorn@uu.nl

MARTIJN HUYSMANS, PhD, is an Assistant Professor in the School of Economics, Utrecht University, The Netherlands. His research is focused on political economy, and he teaches in an interdisciplinary PPE program (politics, philosophy, economics). Email: m.huysmans@uu.nl

SUSANNE C. KNITTEL, PhD, is Assistant Professor of Comparative Literature at Utrecht University. Her research focuses on the cultural representation of violence, trauma, and atrocity. She teaches courses on modern and contemporary literature, literary theory, cultural memory, ecocriticism, and posthumanism. Email: s.c.knittel@uu.nl

BRIANNE MCGONIGLE LEYH, PhD, is Associate Professor of human rights law and global justice. Her research and teaching focuses on conflict and security, international criminal law, transitional justice, victims' rights, and documentation and accountability for serious human rights violations. Email: b.n.mcgonigle@uu.nl

MEREL VAN GOCH, PhD, is Assistant Professor of Liberal Arts and Sciences at Utrecht University, The Netherlands. She is interested in how and what students and scholars learn, especially in interdisciplinary contexts. Her research topics include metacognition, creativity, and other competences relevant to higher education, and her teaching methods emphasize students' self-directed learning. Email: m.m.vangoch@uu.nl

All authors are based at Utrecht University and are members of the Utrecht Young Academy (UYA) at the time of writing. We thank Martine Veldhuizen, Hetty Grunefeld, Esther Slot, and Judith Loopers for their helpful comments and suggestions. Any mistakes or omissions are our own. Email correspondence: T.G.Diphoorn@uu.nl

Manuscript submitted: ***May 15, 2022***
Manuscript revised: ***Sept 28, 2022***
Accepted for publication: ***Oct 15, 2022***

Peer-Reviewed Article

The Market for Kidneys: Bridging Introductory Courses in Economics and Ethics

Martijn Huysmans
School of Economics, Utrecht University, Netherlands

ABSTRACT

This article contributes to the literature on interdisciplinary teaching by describing, analyzing, and evaluating an interdisciplinary intervention while students are still gaining disciplinary grounding. The intervention bridges courses in microeconomics and ethics. It focuses on the travelling concepts of voluntariness and value in a potential market for kidneys and finds that a 15-minute video clip on travelling concepts can help students build interdisciplinary skills. Students in a control group watched a clip only on the specific issue of a market for kidneys, but not using travelling concepts. An exploratory survey (N=44) indicates that the intervention increases interdisciplinary skills more than the control. However, students in the control group reported a deeper interdisciplinary grasp of that specific topic. Teaching an issue through travelling concepts can hence be seen as an investment in general interdisciplinary skills.

Keywords: Interdisciplinarity, Travelling Concepts, Video clip, Economics, Ethics, Value, Voluntariness

INTRODUCTION

There is scant research on but growing interest in interdisciplinary teaching (Klein, 1990; Spelt et al., 2009). One tool used in interdisciplinary research is the idea of travelling concepts (Bal, 2002). I believe, with Bal, that analyzing how concepts are defined and used differently across disciplines is a key way of building interdisciplinary knowledge and skills. Given the dearth of interdisciplinary teaching techniques, a logical question is: are travelling concepts a useful tool to teach interdisciplinary skills? I will try in this paper to answer this question by describing, analyzing, and evaluating an interdisciplinary session on the topic of a market for kidneys. The travelling concepts used in the intervention are value and voluntariness, and the disciplines are economics and ethics.

Interdisciplinary skills are useful for students to overcome the limits of a monodisciplinary perspective. They are often touted as increasingly valuable and necessary in order to solve complex societal problems. In addition, irrespective of problem-solving benefits, they bring intellectual stimulus and satisfaction as they allow students to come to "a more comprehensive understanding" (Newell, 2001: 2).

Literature suggests that the use of video in higher education can bring learning benefits (Noetel et al., 2021). The intervention was delivered through a knowledge clip, i.e. a short video clip explaining one topic. However, the focus of this article is not about evaluating the use of video clips for interdisciplinary teaching. Rather, it is about the use of travelling concepts for interdisciplinary teaching: does a video with travelling concepts work better than one without?

I find that using travelling concepts is indeed useful to build students' interdisciplinary skills in the framework of Rekpo and Szostak (2021). In particular, students gain in perspective taking but also disciplinary grounding: by seeing the differences with another discipline, the nature of each discipline becomes clearer. Travelling concepts are also a useful tool to help students find common ground between different disciplines. Finally, travelling concepts can help students learn about the difficulties of integration when trying to form an opinion or a recommendation on whether we should have a market for kidneys. However, there seems to be some short-run opportunity cost of using travelling concepts in teaching. The control group of the intervention was exposed to an interdisciplinary explanation of the market for kidneys, but without using travelling concepts. This group reported a somewhat better interdisciplinary understanding of the specific issue, but a somewhat smaller increase in general interdisciplinary skills. All in all, the intervention and exploratory survey described in this article suggest that travelling concepts are indeed a useful tool to teach interdisciplinary skills.

LITERATURE REVIEW

Before describing the intervention in more detail and analyzing its results, it is important to have some basic disciplinary knowledge that is used in the intervention. This section provides the necessary disciplinary grounding to understand the challenges and opportunities of the intervention. As we shall see, the concepts of voluntariness and value have different meanings in economics and ethics. They only travel to a certain extent. Where economics has relatively thin conceptions of them, ethics has thicker and more demanding conceptions. This will be important to understand how the intervention using these travelling concepts can help in teaching interdisciplinary skills.

The market for kidneys

Should we have a market for kidneys? The answer to this question has far-reaching implications: in 2014, over 3,000 people died in the US alone while they were waiting for a kidney transplant (Brennan & Jaworksi, 2015: 8). Like most countries in the world, the US bans the sale of kidneys and only allows donations. Markets may help solve the underprovision of kidneys, but at what cost?

Economics teaches us that competitive markets are efficient: they reallocate goods from those with the lowest marginal cost of producing them to those with the highest willingness to pay for them. The prohibition of getting paid for donating a kidney can be considered an extreme price ceiling (at a price of zero), leading to correspondingly extreme efficiency losses: people with a high willingness to pay not getting one, and people who could have made money from their kidneys not getting any (Pindyck & Rubinfeld, 2015: 333-335). Yet many ethicists object to markets in organs. They worry about increasing commodification as we transition from "having a market economy to being a market society" (Sandel, 2013: 10). Specifically, they worry for two sets of reasons. The first is about coercion or weak agency: given economic inequality, poor people might be coerced by their circumstances into selling their kidney. The second is about corruption: by accepting a market for kidneys, do we risk undervaluing the body as a collection of marketable spare parts (Satz, 2008: 279) rather than as something sacred?

It seems that economics as a discipline would favor a market for kidneys, while ethics would be against (although see Brennan & Jaworski: 2015). I argue that these conflicting visions can be understood by considering two travelling concepts: voluntariness and value. These concepts are used in both economics and ethics, but their meanings, while similar, differ in important ways. The different understanding of the concepts clarifies the different judgment on a market for kidneys. For a transaction to be voluntary to an economist is not the same as for an action to be voluntary in the eyes of an ethicist. Similarly, for a commodity to have value to an economist is not the same as for someone to value something in the eyes of an ethicist. Through the prism of these travelling concepts, students can start to appreciate the differences between economics and ethics as disciplines.

Economics: value as the price on a market with voluntary transactions

In economics, the natural way to think about the donation of kidneys is in terms of a market with a price of zero. When the government prohibits the sale of kidneys for money, this can be analyzed as a price ceiling of zero (see e.g. Pindyck & Rubinfeld, 2015: 334). It is a key insight from economics 101 that price ceilings are inefficient, leading to artificial scarcity and black markets.

Markets are the meeting place of supply and demand. The supply curve shows how many units people are willing to sell at any given price. Suppliers are ranked from low to high prices. Based on economic theory of profit maximization, the supply curve of a good is determined by its marginal cost. The more costly it is to produce a good, the higher the price suppliers will require for it. Since one can live with only one kidney, some people may find donating a kidney (almost) without cost. Other people may find it somehow more costly to supply a kidney; perhaps they have high-paying jobs and taking time off for the operation would cost them a lot of money. Or perhaps they have only one kidney that functions properly, so giving one away would cause them significant health costs.

On the other side of the market, the demand curve shows the willingness to pay of consumers. Those with the highest willingness to pay are put first. Based on economic theory of utility maximization, consumers' willingness to pay is equal to the marginal utility from one additional unit of the good. Some people may value a kidney more because they are in more urgent need. Note that basic textbook economics tends to ignore that in reality, people's willingness to pay is limited by their ability to pay. If two people would experience the same increase in happiness from a new kidney (assuming one could measure that), the one with the higher budget will likely have a higher willingness to pay.

Perfectly competitive markets, it is argued in economic textbooks, maximize efficiency due to the voluntary nature of transactions. They do this by making sure that goods are produced and (re)allocated from those who value them least to those who value them most, i.e. up to the point where supply equals demand. The proof of this statement hinges on transactions being voluntary: if A sells something to B for price p, and both A and B agreed on this voluntarily, then it must be the case that B values the good more than p, and A values it less. Hence voluntary transactions by definition increase total wellbeing. Since this process can be assumed to continue until there are no goods allocated to someone that someone else values more, perfectly competitive markets maximize efficiency.

The value of a good, in economics, can be equated to the price prevailing on a market in equilibrium, i.e. a market where the process of voluntary exchange has come to a standstill because there are no more efficiency-enhancing transactions left. The market price has a signal function. The higher it is, the scarcer the good, and hence the more valuable. High prices encourage people not to consume too much of something. In contrast, low prices signal that a good is not very scarce or valuable.

When the market for kidneys is forbidden, this implies a price ceiling of zero. When kidneys can only be exchanged at a price of zero, there are people who would be willing to pay more than zero but not getting a kidney. And there are people who would be willing to sell a kidney who are now not making any money. Hence there will be a welfare loss compared to the market equilibrium.

Talking about a market for kidneys in this matter-of-factly style may feel uncomfortable. Is the sale of a kidney really the same as the sale of an apple, a watch, or a car? The next section documents the reasons ethicists have provided for our unease. At the same time, once one has been trained in economics, it becomes hard not to think of voluntary transactions and value in this way. That is because the idea of a market is a threshold concept (Meyer & Land, 2005; Zepke, 2013): once learned, it becomes hard to un-see it. Relatedly, an interesting feature of concepts is that they function as miniature theories (Bal, 2002: 22). In order to explain the concept properly, one needs to explain the underlying disciplinary theories. It is precisely this feature of concepts that explains why looking at the travelling concepts of voluntariness and value in the market for kidneys can shed so much light on the differences between economics and ethics.

Ethics: voluntariness as positive freedom and value as pluralist

To what extent do the concepts of voluntariness and value travel from economics to ethics? Superficially, they travel well – in line with their meaning in everyday language. However, given more thought, there are crucial differences. Broadly speaking, the concepts seem thicker or richer in ethics, making them – as we shall see – more demanding.

In ethics, it is hard to think of voluntariness without thinking of freedom. In particular, an action is voluntary if it is in line with freedom. Isaiah Berlin (1966) famously distinguished between negative and positive freedom. Negative freedom means being free from outright coercion – not having a gun to your head. Positive freedom means being effectively free to pursue one's goals. It is more in line with virtue ethics or the capabilities approach of Amartya Sen and others. It requires for people to have the means (such as money, time, or education) to thrive and autonomously pursue meaningful goals.

The distinction between negative and positive freedom immediately makes clear where ethicists and economists differ in their idea of voluntariness. In economics, a transaction is voluntary if it is not subject to outright coercion – in effect, economics uses the standard of negative freedom. Ethicists, in contrast, will point out that we could and perhaps should use the higher standard of positive freedom to judge voluntariness. In a very unequal world, the choice set of the poor may be so limited that they effectively have very little or no choice but to sell their kidney. They need to sell their kidney in order to feed their children, for instance. The different standard for a transaction to be voluntary is one key reason for the different opinion of economics and ethics on markets for kidneys.

To wrap up on voluntariness, its travelling from economics to ethics as pleading for markets for kidneys is limited by the ethical objection of coercion. Where economists favor markets because voluntary transactions maximize efficiency, ethicists worry about people being effectively coerced to sell their kidneys at low prices to rich people. In this light, markets for kidneys seem to make the right to health and survival conditional on wealth, rather than markets being a neutral device to maximize efficiency. In other words, ethicists would argue, in the unequal world we are living in, economists conflate willingness to pay and ability to pay.

The second key concept, value, also travels well superficially, but less well in terms of supporting markets. The key reason is the possibility of value being corrupted. Economists see markets as a neutral device of finding out what the value of something is, i.e. how scarce it is when we confront supply and demand. Value then, is a relatively simple and thin concept. It is also contingent: it is not absolute, but determined by where supply and demand happen to meet. Ethicists have a much broader conception of value, allowing for the notion that value can be corrupted. Just as prostitution would desecrate or undervalue sex and marriage, a market for kidneys would corrupt altruistic motives and desecrate the human body.

A seminal work on how the concept of value is different in economics and ethics is Elizabeth Anderson's (1993) book *Value in Ethics and Economics*. In economics value is monistic (of one type) and hence all goods are commensurable: they can be compared on a common scale of value, namely the price on a competitive market. In contrast to the economic and monistic conception of value, Anderson develops a pluralist theory of value: "We care about things and people in different ways, which express […] different modes of valuation, such as love, respect, and admiration" (p. 6). A good is corrupted or a practice is degrading if it values a good according to a lower mode of valuation than it deserves. In particular, human beings are worthy of respect and consideration, rather than being seen as a useful source of kidneys. To the extent that markets would promote the use of lower modes of valuation, they corrupt.

To summarize, the concepts of voluntariness and value have different meanings in economics and ethics. They only travel to a certain extent. Where economics has relatively thin conceptions of them, ethics has thicker and more demanding conceptions. Within the context of the market for kidneys, these differences in conceptualization can make or break the case for allowing a market in kidneys.

The next section on research methods provides the context, discusses the intervention, and presents the motivation and intended objectives.

RESEARCH METHOD

This article focuses on the "the market for kidneys" in the interdisciplinary PPE program at Utrecht University. After having discussed our syllabi of microeconomics and ethics and public policy, we – the teachers of these courses – saw the topic as a natural way to bridge these monodisciplinary first-year courses in an interdisciplinary way. While activities related to the market for kidneys have been part of the program from the beginning, the use of the travelling concepts of voluntariness and value was only tried in the fourth cohort. The focus of this article is to see whether the use of travelling concepts is useful in teaching interdisciplinary skills. Hence a treatment group was exposed to travelling concepts and a control group was not. A survey gives insight on the learning benefits.

Context

In 2018, Utrecht University (UU) launched a bachelor program in Politics, Philosophy, and Economics (PPE) with the addition of History as a fourth discipline. In many ways, the PPE program shows UU's commitment to interdisciplinarity. It was an explicit ambition of the program to not just consist of a multidisciplinary offering of courses to be taken in parallel to each other. Rather, the program is designed to have meaningful interdisciplinary interactions.

The PPE program is selective, admitting only 75 students per year. The program is taught in English, and a majority of students are not from the Netherlands. One of the criteria for admission is that students should at least be open to the four disciplines. Prior courses are not required, but students should be willing to engage with all four disciplines. This means that students are explicitly choosing for an interdisciplinary program.

One way of thinking about depth of interdisciplinarity is Repko & Szostak's (2021) classification. First comes disciplinary grounding: understanding the types of subjects, questions, methods, and concepts used in a given discipline. Next comes perspective taking: being able to take multiple disciplines to bear on one issue. If a program only offers parallel courses in different disciplines, arguably it can never guarantee students moving beyond this second stage. Roughly, the second stage corresponds to the idea of multidisciplinarity (several disciplines in parallel) rather than interdisciplinarity (a meaningful interaction between the disciplines). Third is finding common ground: realizing what the similarities and differences of disciplines are in terms of subjects, questions, methods, and concepts. Finally, there is integration: creating a creative synthesis of the disciplines. This can happen by adding or modifying disciplinary concepts. It is easiest to understand in terms of giving an answer on a question or a recommendation for addressing an issue that takes the different disciplinary insights into account.

The PPE program seeks to take students through the four levels of interdisciplinary skills. In the first year of the program, students are trained in disciplinary grounding. The second quarter of year 1, for instance, has introductory courses in economics (course name: Microeconomics) and philosophy (course name: Ethics and Public Policy). While the focus in year one is on disciplinary grounding, multi- and interdisciplinary bridges are created both throughout the teaching weeks and during a dedicated "step back week". The second year of the program has interdisciplinary courses, co-taught by lecturers from different disciplines. The third year consists of electives and an interdisciplinary thesis.

Towards the end of the courses, the lecturers from both the economics and the ethics course discuss the market for kidneys from their disciplinary perspectives. We make explicit to the students that this is intentional. Our teaching centers on the example of organ shortages as a societal problem requiring an interdisciplinary approach. The economic analysis is centered on the concepts of voluntary transactions, consumer surplus, producer surplus, price ceilings, excess demand, and deadweight loss. The ethics analysis brings in arguments of commodification, corruption of value, dignity, and (economic) coercion. In both courses, the instructors attempt to describe and bring into their own disciplinary world the concepts from the other discipline. After students have been exposed to both the economic and ethical perspectives, there is a classroom debate on the topic.

The author is a lecturer in the economics course. This could be a source of bias. However, this study is about interdisciplinary skills, and not about the importance of economics. In addition, the author has some training in philosophy and discussed the intervention with colleagues from ethics.

Intervention

In 2022, I introduced an intervention with the explicit use of voluntariness and value as travelling concepts. Study participants were the students in the Microeconomics course of the PPE program described above. The course takes place in the second quarter of the first year of this interdisciplinary bachelor's program. Fifty students participated. The majority of students are between 18 and 20 years old. The program is international, with students predominantly from Western European nationalities.

Figure 1. Screenshot from treatment group

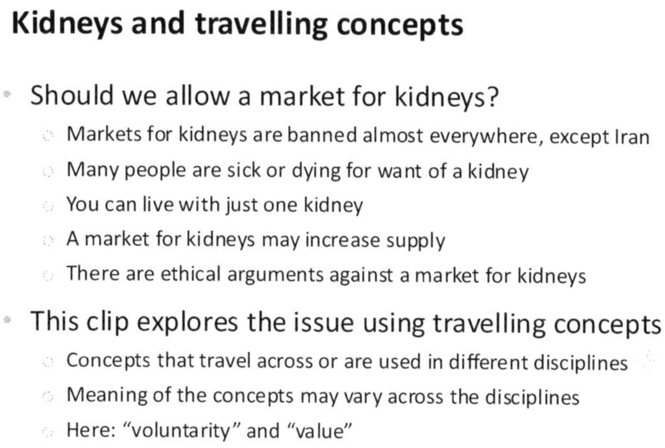

Kidneys and travelling concepts

- Should we allow a market for kidneys?
    - Markets for kidneys are banned almost everywhere, except Iran
    - Many people are sick or dying for want of a kidney
    - You can live with just one kidney
    - A market for kidneys may increase supply
    - There are ethical arguments against a market for kidneys
- This clip explores the issue using travelling concepts
    - Concepts that travel across or are used in different disciplines
    - Meaning of the concepts may vary across the disciplines
    - Here: "voluntarity" and "value"

Figure 2. Screenshot from control group

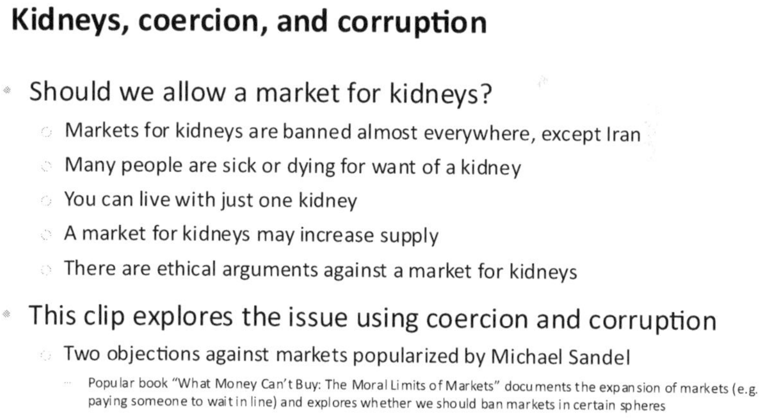

Kidneys, coercion, and corruption

- Should we allow a market for kidneys?
    - Markets for kidneys are banned almost everywhere, except Iran
    - Many people are sick or dying for want of a kidney
    - You can live with just one kidney
    - A market for kidneys may increase supply
    - There are ethical arguments against a market for kidneys
- This clip explores the issue using coercion and corruption
    - Two objections against markets popularized by Michael Sandel
        - Popular book "What Money Can't Buy: The Moral Limits of Markets" documents the expansion of markets (e.g. paying someone to wait in line) and explores whether we should ban markets in certain spheres

Prior to the debate, half of the group watched a short knowledge clip on the market for kidneys making explicit reference to the idea of travelling concepts, and how they can shed light on disciplinary differences. This knowledge clip covered the travelling concepts of value and voluntariness as explained in the literature section. Figure 1 shows a screenshot from this knowledge clip used for the treatment group. The other half watched a knowledge clip of similar length also talking about the economic and ethical perspectives, but not about the notion of the travelling concepts value and voluntariness. Instead, it focused on the objections of coercion and corruption as used by Sandel (2013) against organ markets. Figure 2 shows a screenshot from this knowledge clip used for the control group. Both knowledge clips were recorded by me. Due to the covid pandemic, students watched these clips at home.

Motivation and intended objectives

How can thinking about the market for kidneys and the concepts of voluntariness and value help students develop interdisciplinary skills ranging from disciplinary grounding to interdisciplinary integration? Focusing on a societal problem as an opening to interdisciplinarity is in line with the view of interdisciplinarity being necessary to address complex societal issues. The hope is that picking a real and pressing societal issue will make the motivation of interdisciplinarity more natural, rather than having students perceive it as artificial and purely pedagogical. This relates to the idea of authentic learning (Herrington et al., 2014). Indeed, some students may not see the need to build interdisciplinary skills in general, while they may see the need to address a complex societal issue, which then requires an interdisciplinary approach. This is similar to the use of real-world physics problems to teach and motivate mathematics.

Given the disciplinary outlooks outlined above, it is to be expected that during the ethics class students would be against a market for kidneys, and during the economics class they would be in favor. This may result in confusion or "aporia" (puzzlement), which is productive to the extent that it drives home the point that different disciplinary perspectives may lead to different answers to societal puzzles.

The exercise of perspective taking (switching between the economics and ethics perspectives) may also clarify the epistemologies of the two disciplines. By confronting the disciplines, each discipline's assumptions, theories, and ways of answering questions become clearer. Perspective taking can hence help with disciplinary grounding as well. One can think of this as the idea of signifiers in language being defined in opposition to others. Children learn what a cat is by comparing it to, say a bird (a cat has no wings), a stuffed animal (a cat moves autonomously), or a person (a cat cannot talk). By seeing how ethics and economics approach a market for kidneys and use concepts differently, a similar thing is accomplished: students see more clearly what the disciplines are by understanding their differences.

In addition, students can learn from this puzzlement that disciplines may be incommensurable: solutions or policies may be independently better or worse on disciplinary axes but there is no easy way to come to one unified judgment or metric, i.e. to arrive at interdisciplinary integration. This incommensurability may frustrate some students, but is the goal of (interdisciplinary) education to produce final conclusions and "solutions" (Stoller, 2020), or is it to stimulate critical thinking? Adding ethics next to economics, but also more generally combining disciplines can reduce a fixation on "solutions" and easy answers. Students may also gain increased understanding of and respect for policymakers who have to accomplish the integration of different perspectives into policy decisions.

RESULTS

This section is based on a survey conducted in 2022 after the experiment with travelling concepts. The 25 students in the treatment group watched a knowledge clip called "voluntarity and value", explaining what travelling concepts are and giving the examples of voluntariness and value regarding the market for kidneys. The control group of 25 students watched a knowledge clip called "coercion and corruption" also on interdisciplinarity and the market for kidneys, but not introducing the idea of travelling concepts. Both clips lasted about 15 minutes.

After watching the clips, the students were invited to take a short online survey. The response rate was 88%: 44 out of 50 students filled out the survey (21 from the treatment group and 23 from the control group). Table 1 summarizes the results of three questions on a 1 to 5 scale (disagree to agree):
- *The knowledge clip helped me to come to a well-founded opinion on whether a market for kidneys should be allowed*
- *The knowledge clip helped me to think about the market for kidneys in an interdisciplinary way*
- *The knowledge clip improved my interdisciplinary skills also beyond the market for kidneys*

Table 1: Survey results, average of 1-5 score disagree-agree (*N* = 44)

Item	Control group (*N* = 23)	Travelling concepts (*N* = 21)
Well-founded opinion	3.0	3.1
Interdisciplinarity kidneys	4.4	3.9
Interdisciplinarity beyond kidneys	3.6	3.9

Given the small sample size, no statistical models were run, and the results should be seen as exploratory. From the answers, it seems both clips helped students more or less equally (3.0 versus 3.1 out of 5 on average) to come to a well-founded opinion on whether a market for kidneys should be allowed. The control group felt more strongly (4.4 versus 3.9) that the clip helped them think about the market for kidneys in an interdisciplinary way.

However, the control group also felt less strongly (3.6 versus 3.9) that the clip improved their interdisciplinary skills also beyond the market for kidneys.

Table 2 shows some quotes from both groups in response to the open question "What did you take away from the knowledge clip?". They suggest that indeed students in both groups learned about the market for kidneys from an interdisciplinary point of view combining economics and ethics. However, only students in the treatment group reported on concepts being understood differently in the two disciplines.

Table 2: Takeaways from the knowledge clip

Control group	Travelling concepts
"Kidney markets might lead to the poor being somewhat forced to sell their kidney due to coercion […]"	"different disciplines, in this case philosophy and economics, can have different conceptions of words. […]"
"[…] from an economics standpoint it seems quite clear one should allow kidney markets […] From an ethical standpoint, coercion and corruption play a role."	"[…] it was interesting to briefly hear the difference in how economics vs ethics understand 'value'."

DISCUSSION AND CONCLUSIONS

This article has shown how the travelling concepts of voluntariness and value can be used in the context of the market for kidneys to understand the differences between economics and ethics. Thinking about whether or not a market for kidneys should be allowed motivates and stimulates students to train their interdisciplinary skills.

The concepts of voluntariness and value have different meanings in economics and ethics. They only travel to a certain extent. Where economics has relatively thin conceptions of them, ethics has thicker and more demanding conceptions. For instance, value in economics refers to the equilibrium price on a market with voluntary transactions. In contrast, value in ethics is pluralist, and respect and love are seen as higher modes of valuation than use. Within the context of the market for kidneys, these differences in conceptualization can make or break the case for allowing a market in kidneys.

The article described and analyzed an intervention using the travelling concepts of value and voluntariness in the context of a market for kidneys. The intervention consisted of a 15-minute video clip explaining the idea of travelling concepts and applying it to the example. The study also used a control group, which involved a video clip of equal length but not using the idea of travelling concepts. Both the intervention and the control video clip discussed a potential market for kidneys.

Based on an exploratory survey, it seems that for a given short time investment of 15 minutes, teaching students about travelling concepts is especially helpful at improving their interdisciplinary skills also beyond the specific topic at hand. There may however be a short-run cost in terms of interdisciplinary thinking about the specific issue at hand. However, given the very short amount of time required, it seems like both clips could be combined into one.

Explicitly training students about travelling concepts with a 15-minute clip seems to help them better to develop their interdisciplinary skills than showing them a clip of equal length that only focuses on an interdisciplinary issue without the notion of travelling concepts. However, the latter clip did help students more to think about the issue at hand in an interdisciplinary way, suggesting there is some short-run tradeoff in issue-specific and general interdisciplinary skills. Further experiments and research may try to run similar comparisons in larger groups of students, as well as investigating whether the strong points of both clips could be combined in one clip.

The idea of picking a concrete topic to teach general interdisciplinary skills was motivated by the notion of authentic learning: students are likely to feel more motivated by concrete topics that require an interdisciplinary analysis, than by learning interdisciplinary skills without a real-world application. Since the control group also worked on the same specific topic of a market for kidneys, this study cannot scientifically evaluate the merits of authentic learning. However, based on my perception of students' enthusiasm and engagement, it would appear that the authentic learning approach is indeed valuable, and I plan to continue using it.

Finally, it remains challenging for students to come to a policy recommendation by integrating the two disciplines. Even though this aspect can be frustrating, it was argued that this frustration is productive in making students think about the potential incommensurability of disciplinary insights and move away from a narrow focus on solutions.

REFERENCES

Anderson, E. (1993). *Value in Ethics and Economics.* Cambridge, MA: Harvard University Press.

Bal, M. (2002). *Travelling Concepts in the Humanities: A Rough Guide.* Toronto: University of Toronto Press.

Berlin, I. (1966). *Two concepts of liberty: An inaugural lecture delivered before the University of Oxford on 31 October 1958.* Oxford: Clarendon Press.

Brennan, J. & Jaworski, P.M. (2015). *Markets without Limits: Moral Virtues and Commercial Interests*. New York, NY: Routledge.

Herrington, J., Reeves, T. C., & Oliver, R. (2014). Authentic learning environments. In: J. Spector, M. Merrill, J. Elen, & M. Bishop (Eds.), *Handbook of Research on Educational Communications and Technology* (pp.401-412). New York, NY: Springer.

Klein, J. T. (1990). *Interdisciplinarity: History, theory, and practice*. Detroit, MI: Wayne State University Press.

Meyer, J. H., & Land, R. (2005). Threshold concepts and troublesome knowledge (2): Epistemological considerations and a conceptual framework for teaching and learning. *Higher education*, *49*(3), 373-388.

Newell, W. H. (2001). A Theory of Interdisciplinary Studies. *Issues in Integrative Studies*, *19*(1), 1-25.

Noetel, M., Griffith, S., Delaney, O., Sanders, T., Parker, P., del Pozo Cruz, B., & Lonsdale, C. (2021). Video Improves Learning in Higher Education: A Systematic Review. *Review of Educational Research, 91*(2), 204–236. https://doi.org/10.3102/0034654321990713

Pindyck, R.S. & Rubinfeld, D.L. (2015). *Microeconomics* (8th edition). New York, NY: Pearson.

Repko, A.F. & Szostak, R. (2021). *Interdisciplinary Research: Process and Theory* (4th edition). Thousand Oaks, CA: Sage.

Sandel, M. (2013). *What Money Can't Buy: The Moral Limits of Markets*. New York, NY: Farrar, Straus and Giroux.

Satz, D. (2008). The Moral Limits of Markets: The Case of Human Kidneys. *Proceedings of the Aristotelian Society*, *CVIII*(3), 269–288. https://doi.org/10.1111/j.1467-9264.2008.00246

Spelt, E. J. H., Biemans, H. J. A., Tobi, H., Luning, P. A., & Mulder, M. (2009). Teaching and learning in interdisciplinary higher education: A systematic review. *Educational Psychology Review*, *21*(4), 365–378. https://doi.org/10.1007/s10648-009-9113-z

Stoller, A. (2020). A Case for Critical Interdisciplinarity: Interdisciplinarity As Democratic Education. *Issues In Interdisciplinary Studies, 38*(1–2), 31–56.

Zepke, N. (2013). Threshold concepts and student engagement: Revisiting pedagogical content knowledge. *Active Learning in Higher Education*, *14*(2), 97-107.

MARTIJN HUYSMANS, PhD, is an Assistant Professor in the School of Economics, Utrecht University, The Netherlands. His research is focused on political economy, and he teaches in an interdisciplinary PPE program (politics, philosophy, economics). Email: m.huysmans@uu.nl

Manuscript submitted: ***May 13, 2022***
Manuscript revised: ***August 22, 2022***
Accepted for publication: ***October 15, 2022***

Travelling in the Classroom: Podcasting as an Active-Learning Tool for Interdisciplinarity

Tessa Diphoorn and Brianne McGonigle Leyh
Utrecht University, The Netherlands

ABSTRACT

Interdisciplinarity in the classroom is predominantly championed around a need to address pressing social problems by integrating knowledge from diverse disciplines. But can interdisciplinary teaching take shape without the usual problem-solving frame? And are there new methods/mediums through which to explore interdisciplinarity? These questions have led to new and promising developments related to podcasting, active learning, and interdisciplinarity in the classroom. Through the lens of Travelling Concepts, we reflect on our experiences in the making and using of the podcast series – Travelling Concepts on Air – to better understand interdisciplinarity. We show the value of students not only listening to podcasts as a supplementary means of learning, but also creating podcasts as a form of active learning.

Keywords: podcasting, travelling concepts, active learning, interdisciplinarity, education, reflection

INTRODUCTION

Interdisciplinarity in the classroom is most often championed and designed around a need to address a pressing social problem or complex global challenge, which can only be solved by integrating knowledge from diverse disciplines. But can interdisciplinary teaching take shape without the usual frame of solving problems or addressing complex challenges? And are there new methods or mediums through which to explore interdisciplinarity? These two central questions have framed our collaboration and guided our work and have led to new and promising developments related to podcasting, active learning, and interdisciplinarity in the classroom.

In this article we reflect on our experiences with teaching interdisciplinarity by using podcasting as a learning tool. In line with this special issue, we take Travelling Concepts as the key medium to explore interdisciplinarity. As outlined by Mieke Bal (2002), travelling concepts refers to concepts that 'travel' within and across disciplines and this travelling often impacts the meaning, reach, and operational value of the relevant concept. Through the lens of Travelling Concepts, we have been able to explore interdisciplinarity without first identifying a complex problem to be solved. In order to develop this further, in 2020 we created a podcast series – *Travelling Concepts on Air* – to better understand and elaborate on the notion of travelling concepts and how they are related to interdisciplinarity, both in terms of research and education. In each episode of our podcast series, we focus on a particular concept and invite two scholars from different disciplines to join us and converse about how they use a specific concept. By elaborating on their approaches, experiences, understandings, and assumptions, we aim to uncover the potential 'travelling capacity' of a concept and to gain new insights into disciplinary boundaries.

It was through the making of this podcast series that we, as educators, gained deeper understandings of the promises and pitfalls of interdisciplinarity. The podcast was thus a means by which we were able to better appreciate interdisciplinarity. We were learning by doing and wanted to share this method of active learning with our students. We began using the various episodes in our education in two different ways to allow students to gain more insight into how interdisciplinarity can and cannot work. The first was as supplemental material in a diverse set of classrooms (i.e., listening to the episodes and discussing them in class), and the second was in the form of active learning in our own co-taught interdisciplinary seminars wherein students made their own podcast episodes.

In this article, we reflect on our experiences in the making and using of the podcast series to show how podcasting can be used as a learning tool to understand interdisciplinarity. First, we elaborate on core concepts underpinning our work, including interdisciplinarity, podcasting, and active learning. Next, we explain about the making of the podcast series and using it in the classroom. After presenting our findings, we provide some reflections. We emphasize the importance of intrinsic motivation to look beyond disciplinarity boundaries, the significance of time and support in exploring interdisciplinarity exchanges both for students and teachers, the value of these exchanges being facilitated even outside the scope of a problem-solving frame, the usefulness of examining contestations as well as common ground, and most importantly, the benefits of active learning. One of our main conclusions is that *both* students and teachers better understand interdisciplinarity when they are 'doing' interdisciplinary work. Our findings and reflections directly contribute to various areas of education scholarship including the role of podcasting in education (and interdisciplinarity more specifically); interdisciplinarity beyond the problem-solving frame; and the importance of active learning by both students and teachers.

INTERDISCIPLINARITY, PODCASTING, AND ACTIVE LEARNING

As noted in the introduction to this special issue, while interdisciplinary education is on the rise (Alexander, 2019), there is still much to learn about how interdisciplinarity can be used and taught in various educational settings. However, new scholarship and practice in this area is promising (Ashby & Exter, 2019; Angerer et al., 2021). We have drawn inspiration from our colleagues working with the Interdisciplinary Education Team at Utrecht University who employ a four-stage learning model for stimulating interdisciplinary thinking and learning interdisciplinary skills. This model draws from existing theories on interdisciplinary and cognitive development by Alan Repko and acts as a foundation from which interdisciplinary courses and learning activities can be designed. Below we discuss further how we implemented this model through podcasting and how podcasting can then act as a useful teaching tool, especially for interdisciplinarity.

Podcasting emerged in the early 2000s and is seen as a new digital revolution within aural cultures (Berry, 2016; Markman, 2012; Spinelli and Dann, 2019; Llinares et al., 2018). Podcasts are increasingly used in academia, both for research purposes (Fantini and Buist, 2021) and in education. There is growing research on how podcasts can be used in education, particularly as a means of engaging with students (Fernandez et al., 2015; Heiselen, 2010; Lin et al., 2013; Lee et al., 2008), and there is a prominent focus on the use of podcasting in language learning (Abdous et al., 2012). Advantages of podcasting in teaching have centered on listening (Clark and Walsh, 2004; Dunbridge, 1984), the time-shifting ability, i.e., being able to listen across time and space (Muppala and Kong, 2007), and accessibility (Hew, 2009). Heiselen, for example, argues that 'students experience podcasts as a genuine improvement to the study environment' and that podcasts are good spaces for 'experimentation' (2010: 1063).

In understanding how podcasts can be used in teaching, various categories have been identified (Vogele and Gard, 2006; Rosell-Aguilar, 2007) to differentiate between administrative podcasts (guides), special lecture series (guest lectures), and classroom podcasts (general curriculum teaching and content). Furthermore, podcasts can be used in a substitutional, supplementary, and creative manner (McGarr, 2009). Podcasts are often used in a supplementary way, as a blended learning process wherein they are used alongside other teaching tools. This approach contrasts with more encompassing styles, namely 'inverting the classroom', where all in-class sessions are replaced with podcasts (Gannod, Burge, & Helmick, 2008). As highlighted by Heiselen (2010), much more longitudinal research on the usage and impact of podcasting in teaching is needed, and this article contributes to this growing body of work by exploring how podcasting can be used in interdisciplinary education. For our purposes, we are specifically interested in how podcasting can act as a teaching tool and can contribute to active learning. This means that students not only listen to podcasts as an important supplementary means of learning, but also create the podcasts themselves as a form of active learning.

Over the last few decades, active learning has attracted a good deal of attention in educational scholarship. Influential frameworks for describing the learning process, including Bloom's Taxonomy and the 5E Instructional Model, call for active learning as part of higher order thinking (Bloom et al., 1956; Bybee et al., 2006). For many it is a clear departure from traditional instruction where students passively receive information from a lecture (Hyun et al., 2017). Generally, active learning is defined as any method of learning that engages students directly in the learning process, requiring them to undertake meaningful learning activities and to learn by doing (Bradberry & De Maio, 2019: 94; Bronwell & Eisen, 1991). This entails a process whereby students directly construct knowledge and actively engage with and critically reflect on the subject matter (CAS, 2017). Students acquire knowledge and skills from direct experiences outside of the traditional classroom setting. Often, the active learning is combined with collective or collaborative learning processes (Princ,e 2004). There is extensive empirical support for active learning in the classroom (Prince, 2004; Michael, 2006), with research indicating an increase in content knowledge, critical thinking, and problem solving (Anderson et al., 2005; Kember & Leung, 2005), as well as an increase in an enthusiasm for learning (Hyun et al., 2017; Thaman et al., 2013).

Successful active learning is also important for teachers and the roles they take on (see Cook-Sather, 2011; Morrison, 2014). To achieve successful active learning, Børte et al. (2020) identified three prerequisites that are closely linked to the role of the teacher and broader institutional setting: (1) better alignment between research and teaching practices; (2) a supporting infrastructure for research and teaching; and (3) staff professional development and learning designs. Their work indicates the important relationship between teachers and students, as well as their broader environment. However, much of the literature on active learning and teachers focuses on how teachers can facilitate active learning in the classroom (see

Kudryashova et al., 2016) rather than on the active learning processes of teachers themselves. Our aim, with this article, is to address both points because very often the learning process of the teacher is taken for granted. Accordingly, before we could bring podcasting into the interdisciplinary classroom as an active learning tool for students, we first had to learn by doing it ourselves.

PHASE 1: MAKING THE PODCAST SERIES

To explore interdisciplinarity in the classroom through podcasting, our project included two different phases. The first phase revolved around our own process of learning by doing, i.e., making the podcast series, and the second phase involved using the podcast as a learning tool in education in two different ways.

We are independent and non-professional audio podcasters, and this podcast series was set up through a combination of both personal and professional motives (see Markman, 2012). We met in 2016 as members of the Utrecht Young Academy (UYA), and there was an immediate connection between us. The fist author is an anthropologist and conducts research on violence, security, and policing in South Africa and Kenya. The second author is a legal scholar specializing in international human rights law, transitional justice, international criminal law, and victims' rights. This combination of law and anthropology, along with our friendly relationship, would assist in the informal and spontaneous atmosphere of the podcast. Furthermore, as women, we also wanted to counteract the male dominance within the podcasting world (see Markman, 2012). We explicitly mention our collegial relationship, as we think that this is a key part of how this podcast series, and interdisciplinarity works. As we discuss later, and as shown throughout this special issue, interdisciplinarity often works with people that establish certain understandings and relationships with each other. Our relationship, we argue, was crucial to the setting up and execution of the podcast and the successful use of podcasting in an interdisciplinary classroom.

After the preparatory work that included various technical and logistical issues, we then recorded episodes in a recording studio provided by the university. To minimize the politicization of editing (see Fantini and Buist, 2021), our recording sessions generally do not exceed the 45-minute mark. In Season 1 of the series, we covered nine concepts: *war*, *sustainability*, *time*, *civil society*, *heritage*, *agency*, *legitimacy*, *transformation*, and *diplomacy*. In Season 2, we covered 10 concepts: *sea level*, *surveillance*, *equilibrium*, *security*, *facts*, *sovereignty*, *queer*, *violence*, *youth*, and *crisis*. We knew early on that our audience would be a scholarly/academic one, namely people who like to discuss and think about concepts across disciplinary borders and listen to others doing so. Although it is difficult to ascertain who listens to which podcasts, there is a general observation that podcasts 'attract people who are already somewhat interested in the subjects covered in the podcast they subscribe' (Birch and Weitkamp, 2010: 892).

In developing the podcast series, we structured each episode around five main questions:

1. How did the concept originate (in your discipline) and how do you use it in your research?
2. Are you aware of the ways in which other disciplines approach the concept?
3. How are the various usages complementary?
4. Where is the friction in the various usages of the concept?
5. What are ways to move forward?

These questions were intended to prepare our guests for the conversation, although bearing in mind that discussions often take their own course, and the questions get weaved in and out throughout the conversation. These five questions are aligned to the four-stage learning model used at Utrecht University, which is based on Repko's work, namely: disciplinary grounding, perspective taking, finding common ground, and integration. The first stage of the model – disciplinary grounding – provides the foundation for interdisciplinary understanding (Miller and Boix Mansilla, 2004).

To start the substantive part of the show, we ask the guests a two-part question: how did the concept originate (in their discipline) and how do they use it in their research? The disciplinary grounding element of our show has two key functions. First, very practically, it gives the guests a basis from which to start the discussion. Even if they are engaged in interdisciplinary research and teaching, they likely first worked with the concept when they were carrying out more disciplinary work. Moreover, it is a comfortable question to ease them into the conversation and in almost all the episodes, the guests had a clear starting point from which to begin engagement with the concept. This could be the start of their studies or the commencement of a new research project, showing the temporal differences in terms of how long or in what ways the academics have worked with a particular concept.

Second, by starting with disciplinary grounding, it gives listeners, many of whom are students, a basis from which to understand how the guests work with a concept. Because we invite scholars from a variety of disciplines, it positions them on the academic disciplinary spectrum. Thus far, we have invited scholars from anthropology, chemistry, conflict studies, criminology, earth sciences, economics, ethics/philosophy, governance, history, physics, literary studies, law, psychology, and sociology. Each of these disciplines has its own *perspective* or distinctive way of seeing things that is 'based on commitment to a system of theories, a body of professional knowledge [...]

or a discourse community' (Miller and Boix Mansilla, 2004: 4). By making this clear, guests and listeners are better positioned in the later discussion around interdisciplinary understandings around the concept.

After grounding the concept in two separate disciplines, we often ask the guests—if not already offered voluntarily: Are you aware of the ways in which other disciplines approach the concept? This question is all about perspective taking. In interdisciplinary studies, perspective taking theory is the ability to look at a certain phenomenon, issue, problem, or *concept* from the perspective of another discipline and then being able to identify similarities and differences between them (McElreavy, 2016). For the purposes of the podcast, it is not only valuable for both guests and listeners to realize that there are different opinions about a concept, but also that such understandings can lead to new insights. We especially want listeners to understand how incorporating other disciplinary perspectives can be a way of enriching one's own understanding and/or positioning of a concept (Carmichael, 2018).

The third stage, following perspective taking, is about finding common ground and contestation, and the third and fourth questions focus on that. These questions allow the guests to expand upon their perspective taking exercises. According to Repko and Szostak (2021), a key step in getting to integration for purposes of interdisciplinary learning is finding common ground between disciplines. Yet, because we are interested in both the promises and pitfalls of interdisciplinarity, we were interested in hearing about commonalities as well as contestations. In terms of travelling concepts, this is where a concept or conceptual understanding may or may not have travelled for a particular reason.

In the final and crucial step towards greater interdisciplinarity, integration is key. Integration is about combining disciplinary insights and understandings to develop something new that would have been unachievable through single or even multi-disciplinary means (Miller and Boix Mansilla, 2004). While the podcast does not really aim for integration of perspectives between the guests, we do ask: What are ways to move forward? Through this question, we have sought to move past the commonalities and contestations, to get the views of the guests on new areas of research. Ideally, however, the podcast series can act as a bridge and tool for students to engage in integration, as we discuss below.

Through our guiding questions for the conversations within the podcast that were aligned to the four-stage learning model for interdisciplinary, we, as researchers and educators, learned a great deal about both podcasting as a tool and about interdisciplinarity – this was our own way of learning-by-doing. The next phase centered around using podcasting in the classroom.

PHASE 2: USING THE PODCAST SERIES

We implemented the podcast series in the classroom to teach students about interdisciplinarity in two ways. The first was as a supplementary tool, wherein we requested teachers to assign the various podcast episodes in their classes and then invited their students to fill in a short survey. As a result, across very diverse settings, namely in courses taught in different faculties, in different educational programs, and with students from different levels and exposure to interdisciplinarity, students listened to an episode alongside other required readings. For example, the episode on Sustainability was used in an undergraduate anthropology course on 'Anthropology and Sustainability', and the episode on Civil Society was used in a law module on 'Civic Space and Civil Society'. As a result, the students who filled in the survey had diverse disciplinary backgrounds and levels of experience and expertise.

The survey consisted of the following ten questions:

1. Which episode(s) have you listened to?
2. Did you find the podcast useful in improving your understanding of that particular concept? (if you listened to more than one episode, please make a generalisation across the podcast series)
3. Were you familiar with the idea of a 'travelling concept' before listening to the episode?
4. If 'yes' to question 3, how and where?
5. What do you think of the idea of travelling concepts?
6. Were you familiar with what interdisciplinarity entails before listening to the episode?
7. If 'yes' to question 6, in what ways did you become familiar with interdisciplinarity?
8. How did this podcast shape your ideas on what interdisciplinarity is or can be?
9. What do you think about the use of podcast episodes in teaching?
10. How would you compare listening to a podcast versus reading an article/book chapter for a course?
11. Do you have any additional feedback?

To ensure that it was not too time consuming for the students, the survey consisted of 10 simple questions that focused on knowing more about prior knowledge on traveling concepts and interdisciplinarity and the role of podcasting as a teaching tool, both more generally and specifically for interdisciplinarity. The last open question was meant to provide space for further explanatory dimensions that we may have overlooked. At the time of writing, a total 53 students filled in the survey. Despite the low response, we were able to gain quite some insight into their experiences, as we will discuss in the following section. Furthermore, we will continue to use this survey in the future with similar and new courses and this will allow us to continue collecting data about students' experiences.

The second way we utilized the podcast in education was through a four-week honors seminar series on interdisciplinarity, which we co-taught together. At Utrecht University, we have various programs for honors students at the undergraduate and graduate level. At the master's level, one program is the Graduate Honours Interdisciplinary Seminars (GHIS), which is an extracurricular program that is open for master students across the entire university who are looking for a unique intellectual exchange. In the academic year of 2021-2022, we were invited to organize one of these seminar series, which included four seminars wherein we explored our experiences of interdisciplinarity. In the first two seminars, we focused on our interdisciplinary research experience and how our interactions with one another within the Utrecht Young Academy and Transformative Policing Research Group led to our making of the podcast.

In the third and fourth seminars we focused on the podcast series. As preparation for the third seminar, we asked the students to first listen to some of the episodes (they got to choose) and reflect on the disciplinary grounding that took place, the perspective taking, and whether guests were able to find common ground and, in some cases, share examples of integration—essentially using the Repko approach to interdisciplinarity. During the third seminar, we extensively discussed the various stages within the different episodes in the classroom. With the consent of the students, we recorded and transcribed this conversation, in order to capture their experiences.

In the second half of the third seminar, we implemented a 'Travelling Concepts' pressure cooker, as a starting point for their assignment, i.e. making a podcast episodes. This pressure cooker is an intense (time constrained) session where the students were split into pairs and then, based on their different disciplinary backgrounds, asked to select, and discuss a concept where they could see 'travelling' possibly occurring. We purposely paired students up from different faculties, so that they were really coming from different disciplinary backgrounds. During this pressure cooker of 20 minutes, the students selected a particular concept that they would create an episode on. In total we had 10 students and thus five different pairs and concepts. The homework was then to make a short episode of maximum 15 minutes discussing how their disciplines view and use a certain concept and explore whether there is any common ground. We provided the students with material and support on how to make the podcast. We were thus not only getting the students to listen to podcasts on travelling concepts and interdisciplinarity but asking students to actively make a podcast recording and go through the exercise of an interactive dialogue with their peer.

Eventually, the students produced five episodes on the following concepts: *resilience, consciousness, environment, memory,* and *uncertainty*.

During the fourth seminar, we listened to the episodes together and discussed both the process and content together. The students then helped select which student podcast would be included in our Christmas Special for Travelling Concepts on Air. In the following sections, we draw from our experiences in making the podcast series, our discussions with these students, and the results from the surveys and class evaluations to outline some of our findings on using podcasting to explore interdisciplinarity in the classroom.

FINDINGS

In this section, we discuss our findings for the two different phases of our project, focusing on both teachers and students.

Learning for teachers
Our first key finding is that it is crucial for teachers to undergo a process of active learning themselves. Through the four-stage learning model that outlined the format of our discussions in each of our episodes, we were able to, together with our guests, identify how interdisciplinarity can and cannot work. The discussions we had, as well as the reflections we have had since then, have been pivotal for our own development and learning as educators. Without our own process of active learning, we would not have been able to teach students certain underlying processes about interdisciplinarity or about skills around podcasting.

In terms of disciplinary grounding, we could see that most guests found the second part of the disciplinary grounding question (how they use the concept in their research) relatively easy to answer. Interestingly, the first part of the question (the origins of the concept in their discipline) was not always self-evident. For example, during the episode on Surveillance, both guests were not sure about how the concept had emerged in their own disciplines. We provide the guests with the questions in advance of recording, and by doing so, this has triggered several guests to carry out independent research into the origins of the relevant concept in their fields of study. One of our legal scholars in the episode on War, for example, explicitly mentioned that she had to dig into legal archives to see how the concept originated in her field, and other guests had similar remarks. Furthermore, many mentioned that they had never thought about the origin of a concept in their field before. This is not because they had not been interested but because it had never occurred to them to question the origins of a concept as used in their own discipline. Additionally, with some concepts, the disciplinary origin was not always known. With the concept of legitimacy, for instance, both scholars (from governance and sociology), were not certain about the disciplinary origin, perhaps pointing to the fact that some concepts are used by various disciplines at the outset and not necessarily grounded from a specific discipline.

The next step, of perspective taking, was probably the most important component of the podcast series and it was enlightening to see this happening during the conversations we had. Perspective taking allows the guests, as well as the listeners, to better appreciate the complexity around so-called 'simple concepts'. What we have experienced in the episodes regarding perspective taking has been quite varied. Some guests have indeed thought deeply about how other disciplines have engaged with a concept and drew from those perspectives in their own work. During the episode on Legitimacy, the two scholars from governance and sociology were very aware of the perspectives from other disciplines and drew heavily from them in their own work. Other scholars, such as those from the episodes on War and Transformation, noted understandings from other fields but found them problematic. For the episode on Transformation, while the underlying aspects of the concept were relevant, the term itself had not entered the economic disciplinary sphere. Here, it was clear when limitations of travelling occurred and why. More often, however, after hearing about the guest's perspective taking, conversations lead to discussions about common ground and contestations.

With regards to common ground and contestations, we essentially saw one of three general outcomes: (i) there was a good deal of common ground and understanding between the perspectives; (ii) there was some common ground between the perspectives of the guests; or (iii) there was little common ground. In the episode on Civil Society, for instance, we had guests from law and conflict studies. These are two closely aligned fields of study and the guests had previously worked together in both research and teaching. The discussions showed a good deal of common ground, including the use of common literature sources, theories, and understandings. However, key distinctions were still made clear, thereby showing that full integration may not be achievable or desirable given the divergent audiences of the guests. In the episode on Sustainability, the guests, from anthropology and earth sciences, had some common ground between the ways in which they worked with the concept, such as definitional understandings and literature sources, but departed sharply in terms of how they approach their research more broadly. The anthropologist was much more engaged with critical scholarship whereas the earth scientists/futurist seemed more of a challenged-based scholar—acknowledging the critique, yet more focused on addressing problems and providing solutions. Finally, an example of where little common ground was apparent was the episode on Agency where we invited scholars from law and ethics/philosophy. The conversation was rich and insightful, and the scholars recognized the other field's contributions; yet there was little overlap or common ground.

In terms of contestations, there were less obvious tensions between disciplines. This was largely since many of our guests are actively involved in interdisciplinary research and education. Nevertheless, some tensions did come out. In the episode on Heritage, the two guests, one from anthropology and the other an historian, seemed to have a good deal of common ground between their understandings of the concept. However, both were frustrated by and critical towards the way legal processes and frameworks shape the concept. As such, the tensions highlighted were not between the disciplines represented by the guests but rather a third discipline identified by both guests (and represented by the second author). In the episode on War, there was a clear dispute about the usage of the concept: whilst the legal scholar argued that the notion of 'conflict' is more productive than 'war' since a finding of international armed conflict triggers specific legal obligations and protections, the conflict studies analyst was a proponent of using the phrase and concept of 'war' more broadly to understand contemporary realities around armed violence. The relevance and impact of the concept, as well as the meaning, were points of contestation here.

As we had hypothesized before making the podcast series, most episodes did not result in integration. The episode where integration was most evident was that on Sea Level. In this episode, the two guests discussed explicitly how they came together due to a specific problem (i.e., knowledge-gap) and that due to their different disciplines, they were able to reach new academic insights and practical solutions. Through their collaboration, they were able to reach entirely new ways of measuring and defining sea level – i.e., integration.

By making the podcast series, and thus having these discussions, we, as researchers and teachers, learned a great deal about interdisciplinarity (elaborated below in the section on reflections). We were able to identify the four-stage learning model and these experiences were crucial for us to implement this within our teaching. Furthermore, we also argue that this was due to us working together as an interdisciplinary team. Ample research has shown how team teaching can be effective in education (see Self and Baek, 2017), and we argue that interdisciplinary teaching teams are beneficial for an interdisciplinary classroom.

Learning for students
With regards to learning for students, our first set of findings concern the use of podcasting as a passive learning tool. As discussed, the episodes from our podcast series were firstly used in a supplementary manner, often used as compulsory listening next to other required readings. Several students highlighted a preference for listening to a podcast rather than only reading articles. This was indeed due to the flexibility podcasts offer, i.e., being able

to understand content in a more flexible manner, as highlighted in the following quotes:

> I really enjoyed it... it helped for me to focus only on audio. I listened to it while taking a walk outside, and it was a really wonderful way of learning.
>
> I think it is a good addition to the usual methods because you can do it from anywhere and still receive the information necessary. It is also nice to be able to pause and rewind ;).
>
> I think, listening to a podcast doesn't really feel like an assignment for school, which makes it more fun to learn while listening to it.
>
> Big fan! It's something different in-between all the reading and I can do some work while going on a walk outside.

Some of these sentiments were also echoed by our honor students, especially the time-shifting ability, and thus the ability to rewind, pause, and listen again. Yet, despite the general enthusiasm, a few students also indicated that they preferred books and/or articles and at times were more easily distracted while listening. One student highlighted:

> I think I am more of a visual learner, so I do remember slightly more from reading, but at this time I am always on my computer so it was good to change from always reading to listening.

Another issue that particularly emerged from our discussion with the honor students, and which largely also comes from the format of our podcast series, is the potential for interaction and dialogue. Although podcasts vary in format, ranging from interviews, to storytelling, to investigate journalism, most podcasts center around interaction between two or more individuals. This is limited in academic texts: although scholars often position themselves within a particular debate or field within a scholarly text, the interaction is not live, and we are not immediately exposed to comments and reactions. A podcast provides a space where immediate responses can be voiced. This element of interaction is also crucial to the process of perspective taking. Like other forms of social media, with podcasts there is space for feedback. However, unlike other science-based podcasts, we have not used integrated online discussion forums (IODFs) for further feedback and discussion (Birch and Weitkamp, 2010). Yet our research so far does show promising results, indicating that students enjoy podcasting, particularly as a supplementary tool in their courses.

In addition to podcasting acting as a learning tool more generally, we also wanted to know more about how it is a learning tool for interdisciplinarity more specifically. Although one student mentioned that the podcast: 'just furthered my knowledge on sustainability, not on interdisciplinary', most students did emphasize that the podcast helped them understand how interdisciplinarity works. The podcast introduced many of the students to the notion of travelling concepts. While students had an inherent understanding that concepts travel, they had not been exposed to that phrase as such. One student noted: 'I was not familiar with the term "travelling concept", but I did notice during my reading that some words mean different things across disciplines'. Other students noted:

> I have studied international law, international political science and international economics and have often encountered situations in which one concept meant completely different things in different disciplines - the idea of travelling concepts is thus absolutely crucial for interdisciplinary work in order to avoid misunderstandings.

> Just brilliant! Really contributes to bridging the communication gap multi/interdisciplinary scholarship/work.

In some of the comments from the survey, there was a clear engagement with the four-stage learning model. Several students highlighted how the episodes allowed them to listen to and identify the process of perspective taking, as can be seen from the following quotes from the survey:

> I liked that [the concept of] civil society was not simply discussed from various perspectives, but that you were trying to find a common understanding of the term.

> A podcast is more interactive since it is not just one point of view, you're receiving information from. It is mostly a conversation where we get to know different perspectives which I think is great.

Due to the format of the series, i.e., the conversation with different guests, students who filled in the survey were able to identify perspective-taking. Therefore, podcasting, used in a supplementary way, allowed students to identify the four-stage learning model and thus the potential stages of interdisciplinarity.

With our honor students, this was also the case: podcasting served as a useful learning tool. Yet with them, this was even more the case due to the centrality of active learning, i.e., making an episode themselves. During the discussions we had with the students, they all expressed how much they enjoyed listening to the podcast. As one of them sated in their evaluation form of our GHIS seminars:

> The podcast assignment was also a massive deviation from anything I had previously done and the chance to use to UU podcasting room equally really made this a much more special experience that I would definitely recommend to others.

In addition, they also explicitly mentioned how the episodes helped them understand interdisciplinarity, especially the processes of disciplinary grounding and perspective taking. It was the last two stages, namely finding a common ground and integration, that they experienced as more difficult. Although they recognize that this is the goal, as highlighted by one student: 'That it is an ongoing conversation between different disciplines to create a consensus or an integration of ideas', students found it difficult to execute this themselves. Even though they all were able to find some type of common ground, this did not always feel natural. One pair of honors students, for example, highlighted that they had to have several conversations to really identify where there was a mutual understanding.

The students highlighted that although it was rather challenging to make the podcast episode, it was also rewarding and provided them with a deeper understanding of both the concept, as well as the way interdisciplinarity works. As a result: by having to find a concept, think about disciplinary grounding, having conversations together, and putting together a podcast, i.e., learning by doing, they were able to learn more.

DISCUSSION AND REFLECTIONS

Through the survey and our own experimentation with co-teaching the seminars, we realized that using podcasts in teaching can be a very helpful tool for students to learn more about interdisciplinarity. Many of the results of the survey confirmed some of our initial thoughts and assumptions about the use of podcasts as supplementary material. For instance, an overwhelming number of students found the podcasts useful for understanding a particular concept from different perspectives. This is something that we expected to see in the results of the survey since our own understandings of certain concepts had been enriched while making the podcast.

With regards to interdisciplinarity, the views are more varied. From the survey, namely from those students who had listened to one or two episodes in their courses, it was not that apparent that the episodes were useful to understanding interdisciplinarity. However, from the honor students, this was more the case, and we conclude that this is due to the method of active learning. We saw that when the students were tasked with creating a particular product, there was a heightened sense of understanding and enthusiasm. This finding is in line with research done, across disciplines, on active learning in the classroom (Michael 2006; Prince 2004), with research indicating an increase in content knowledge, critical thinking, and problem solving (Anderson et al., 2005; Kember and Leung, 2005), as well as an increase in an enthusiasm for learning (Thaman et al., 2013).

In line with this, we also conclude that active learning is equally important for teachers. By making this podcast series, we gained a deeper understanding about how interdisciplinarity can and cannot work and this was crucial for our own teaching. In addition, we also identified some other issues during our experiences of experimenting with podcasting, as a way of understanding interdisciplinarity, and using podcasts within education. The first is the importance of *passion or intrinsic motivation* to engage with others across disciplinary boundaries. From our conversations, with colleagues and students, a key factor in successful interdisciplinary collaborations has been a curiosity to learn from or interact with someone from outside their field or discipline (Angerer et al., 2021). There are scholars (and students) who may not see the merit of interdisciplinary engagement and prefer to solely interact with their disciplinary peers. That is fine. Disciplinary studies are also incredibly valuable. However, we believe that for students in particular, exposure to other disciplines already from their bachelor studies is important. It may ignite a passion or curiosity to learn from and engage with others.

Next, we noticed the importance of *time* in fostering successful interdisciplinary collaboration or exchanges. As highlighted by multiple guests, 'it takes time' to really understand other scholars and their usages of a different concept. The first example is our own friendly relationship: we invested time in our partnership in both making the podcast and in using it in education together for our own journey of understanding interdisciplinarity. With the heavy workload inherent to academia, many scholars may have the motivation to interact across borders but simply lack the time to have such discussions. This was beautifully evident in the episode on Time, which included a literary scholar and a geologist. They shared how they, through various collaborations in education, started with perspective taking and only after many conversations and interactions moved onto common ground and even integration, developing their own categories and tools to analyze time. They shared how they still experience new breakthrough moments where their understanding of each other's perspectives increases. As one of them recalled during our session: 'And I remember, we had this epiphany and I look at [name], and... oh, no, I don't think I understood you until now. I think I just got what you mean by that. And that's so interesting!' Similarly, students may be so bogged down in their demanding study programs to take the time to engage with peers across disciplines. For this reason, opportunities like the GHIS for students or similar programs for teachers, such as the UYA or interdisciplinary research groups, are so important. University funding and policies should create spaces and opportunities for teachers and students to experiment with interdisciplinarity through different types of assignments and means of assessment. This finding further supports the research carried out by Børte et al. (2020) on the importance of supportive infrastructures.

Through our podcast and interactions with guests and later with students, we noticed that very often people think that interdisciplinarity only takes place to solve a problem. This is because interdisciplinarity is often promoted in this way—as a means through which to address global challenges that require 'out of the box' and integrated ways of thinking. However, we have found that interdisciplinary exchange is also valuable on a more conceptual level—even when not looking to solve problems. Using the four-stage learning model for stimulating interdisciplinary thinking, we were able to delve in the different goals or approaches scholars taken when thinking about, working with and teaching specific concepts. In the episode on Sustainability, for example, one guest clearly had a problem-solving mentality while the other scholar focused more on critiquing and conceptual thinking. Both found the podcast discussion fruitful. With the episode on Heritage, one of the guests was actively engaged as a practitioner, working with several foundations on issues pertaining to conserving heritage sites, while the other did not. Again, the conversation was appreciated by both as it gave them an opportunity to interact without needing to necessarily solve a problem. We hope that our guests (and students) see these exchanges as a valuable source of inspiration and to enrich one's own understanding and approach—whether that be problem-solving, critical, or conceptional. Overall, we feel that it is important for universities, teachers, and students to value interdisciplinary learning beyond the problem-solving frame.

Another takeaway that we had from our experiences with podcasts and interdisciplinarity, which we also tried to bring out in classroom discussions, is about the level of contestation between the disciplinary exchanges. Very often teaching interdisciplinarity focuses too much on common ground and integration. But contestations and a lack of travelling are equally important to understand and even value in some cases. Here we found the *scope of a discipline and its relation to each other* as a crucial factor in better understanding interdisciplinarity. Sometimes it felt like friction was more likely to occur between scholars who came from rather similar fields. This was evident in the episode on War: although from different fields, the two fields (international humanitarian law and conflict studies) are closely related. One guest was advocating for the use of the concept of war, while the other was not. Due to the closeness of their fields, this divergent viewpoint mattered, as it would impact how other scholars working in their field view and understand their work. With very contrasting disciplines who may not encounter one another, it seems like difference was more easily accepted and even provided a space to allow for pure curiosity-driven exchanges. For example, in the episode on Equilibrium, with a chemist and economist, there were fundamental differences and similarities. Yet, because their perspectives on the notion of equilibrium will not impact the other, the scope for differences was experienced as interesting and not potentially confrontational; it is not something that they would have to address in their work. We saw a similar case with one of the student pairs. Although from different faculties (Science and Social Science), the science student had a background in the social sciences as well, and it was thus rather easy for him to make the disciplinary shift. His disciplinary grounding was thus more diverse and in line with that of his counterpart. This allowed them to find common ground more easily and collaborate.

Finally, reflecting on our experiences, we realize how much we have been learning while doing both in the making of the podcast and in our teaching. Active learning is not just important for students. It is equally important for teachers. Actively experimenting with podcasting and podcasting in education, around interdisciplinarity, has made us better scholars and educators. And, just as with students, reflection is a key part of any active learning process. There are many things that we would also do differently. For example, because we were largely drawing on our own university network, the selection of our guests could have been more diverse. There is a large scope for awareness and improvement here and something we are taking on board for season 3. For us, podcasting has unquestionably been a 'fun and enjoyable activity' (Markman, 2012: 557): in addition to expanding our knowledge on certain concepts and the dimension of travelling, it has also been a way for us to engage across disciplines and has given further insight into the everyday workings of academia.

CONCLUDING REMARKS

When we started, our aim was to do a few episodes and see how things went. We never imagined that so many scholars and students would find our conversations useful. At the time of writing, we have over 5800 downloads, and as also discussed by Markman (2012), were thrilled by the positive feedback we received. We are now looking into a possible third season and hope to share our experiences around podcasting, interdisciplinarity, and teaching with other teachers and educators beyond the geographic borders of the Netherlands. We believe there are boundless possibilities around podcasting as a method of teaching and learning how to do interdisciplinarity and hope to see it grow as a teaching tool in the years to come.

REFERENCES

Abdous, M., Facer, B.R., & Yen, C.J. (2012). Academic effectiveness of podcasting: A comparative study of integrated versus supplemental use of podcasting in second language classes. *Computers & Education, 58*(1), 43-52.

Alexander, B., et al. (2019). *Horizon report 2019 higher education edition.* EDUCAUSE 19. Website https://library.educause.edu/ /media/files/library/2019/4/2019horizonreport.pdf.

Anderson, W.L., Mitchell, S.M., & Osgood, M.P. (2005). Comparison of student performance in cooperative learning and traditional lecture-based biochemistry classes. *Biochemistry and Molecular Biology Education, 33*(6), 387-393.

Angerer, E., Brincker, L., Rowan, E., Scager, K., & Wiegant F. (2021). *Interdisciplinary Orientation. Learning to navigate beyond your discipline.* Utrecht: Utrecht University.

Ashby, I. & Exter, M. (2019). Designing for Interdisciplinarity in Higher Education; Considerations for Instructional designers. *TechTrends, 63*, 202-208.

Bal, M. (2002). *Travelling Concepts in the Humanities. A Rough Guide.* Toronto: University of Toronto Press.

Berry, R. (2016). Podcasting: Considering the evolution of the medium and its association with the word 'radio'. *The Radio Journal International Studies in Broadcast and Audio Media, 14*(1): 7-22.

Birch, H. & Weitkamp, E. (2010). Podologues: conversations created by science podcasts. *New Media & Society, 12*(6), 889-909.

Bloom, B., Englehart, M., Furst, E., Hill, W., & Krathwohl, D. (1956). *Taxonomy of educational objectives: The classification of educational goals. Handbook I: Cognitive domain.* NY, Toronto: Longmans, Green.

Børte, K., Nesje, K. & Lillejord, S. (2020). *Barriers to student active learning in higher education, Teaching in Higher Education.* Website https://doi.org/10.1080/13562517.2020.1839746.

Bradberry, L.A. & De Maio, J. (2017). Learning By Doing: The Long-Term Impact of Experiential Learning Programs on Student Success. *Journal of Political Science Education, 15*(1), 94-111.

Bronwell, C.C., & Eison, J.A. (1991). Active Learning: Creating Excitement in the Classroom. *ASHEERIC Higher Education Rep*ort No. 1

Bybee, R.W., Taylor, J.A., Gardner, A., Van Scotter, P., Powell, J.C., Westbrook, A., & Landes, N. (2006). *The BSCS 5E Instructional Model: Origins, Effectiveness and Applications.* Colorado Springs BSCS.

Carmichael, Tami S. (2018). Global Perspective-Taking: Extending Interdisciplinary Pedagogies into International Classrooms. *English Faculty Publications, 26*(2), 144-166.

Clark, D., & Walsh, S. (2004). *iPod-learning. [White paper].* Epic Group.

Council for the Advancement of Standards in Higher Education (CAS) and by the National Society for Experiential Education as cited in: Minnesota State University. (2017). *Experiential Education: Internships and WorkBased Learning. A Handbook for Practitioners and Administrators.* Website https://www.minnstate.edu/system/asa/workforce/docs/experiential_learningv4.pdf

Cook-Sather, A. (2011). Lessons in Higher Education: Five Pedagogical Practices that Promote Active Learning for Faculty and Students. *The Journal of Faculty Development, 3*, 33-39.

Durbridge, N. (1984). *Media in course design, No. 9, audio cassettes. The role of technology in distance education.* Kent, UK: Croom Helm.

Fantini, E. & Buist, E. (2021). Searching for the Sources of the Nile through a podcast: what did we find? *JCOM, 20*(02), N01. https://doi.org/10.22323/2.20020801.

Fernandez, V., Sallan, J. M., & Simo, P. (2015). Past, present, and future of podcasting in higher education. In *Exploring learning & teaching in higher education*, pp. 305-330. Springer, Berlin, Heidelberg.

Gannod, G.C., Burge, J.E., & Helmick, M.T. (2008). *Using the Inverted Classroom to Teach Software Engineering.* Proceedings of the 30th International Conference on Software Engineering.

Heilesen, S.B. (2010) What is the academic efficacy of podcasting? *Computers & Education, 55*(3), 1063-1068.

Hew, K.F. (2009) Use of audio podcast in K-12 and higher education: A review of research topics and methodologies. *Educational Technology Research and Development, 57*(3), 333-357.

Hyun, J., Ediger, R., & Lee, D. (2017). Students' Satisfaction on Their Learning Process in Active Learning and Traditional Classrooms. *International Journal of Teaching and Learning in Higher Education, 29*(1) 108-118.

Kember, D. & Leung, D.Y.P. (2005). The influence of active learning experiences on the development of graduate capabilities. *Studies in Higher Education, 30*(2), 155-170.

Kudryashova, A., Gorbatova, T., Rybushkina, S. & Ivanova, E. (2016). Teacher's Roles to Facilitate Active Learning, *Mediterranean Journal of Social Sciences, 17*(1), 460-466.

Lee, M.J., McLoughlin, C. & Chan, A. (2008). Talk the talk: Learner-generated podcasts as catalysts for knowledge creation. *British Journal of Educational Technology, 39*(3), 501-521.

Lin, S., Zimmer C., & Lee, V. (2013). Podcasting acceptance on campus: The differing perspectives of teachers and students. *Computers & Education, 68*(1), 416-428.

Llinares, D., Fox, N., & Berry, R. (2018). *Podcasting: New Aural Cultures and Digital Media.* New York: Palgrave Macmillan.

Markman, K.M. (2012). Doing radio, making friends, and having fun: Exploring the motivations of independent audio podcasters. *New Media & Society, 14*(4), 547-565.

McElreavy, C. (2016). Perspective Taking Theory in Interdisciplinary Studies', 4 April 2016. Website https://christinemcelreavy.wordpress.com/2016/04/04/perspective-taking-theory-in-interdisciplinary-studies/.

McGarr, O. (2009). A Review of Podcasting in Higher Education: Its Influence on the Traditional Lecture. *Australasian Journal of Educational Technology*, *25*(3), 309-321.

Michael, J., (2006). Where's the Evidence that Active Learning Works? *Advances in Physiology Education*, *30*, 159-167.

Miller, M. & Boix Mansilla, V. (2004). Thinking Across Perspectives and Disciplines. *Interdisciplinary Studies Project, Project Zero*, Harvard Graduate School of Education. Website http://www.interdisciplinarystudiespz.org/pdf/Miller-VBM_ThinkingAcross_2004.pdf.

Morrison, C.D. (2014). From 'Sage on the Stage' to 'Guide on the Side'. *International Journal for the Scholarship of Teaching and Learning*, *8*(1), 1-15.

Muppala, J. K., & Kong, C. K. (2007). Podcasting and its use in enhancing course content. In V. Uskov (Ed.), *Proceedings of Computers and Advanced Technology in Education*. Beijing, China.

Prince, M., (2004). Does Active Learning Work? A Review of the Research. *Journal of Engineering Education*, *93*(3), 223-231.

Repko, A.F. & Szostak, R. (2021). *Interdisciplinary Research: Process and Theory*, 3rd ed. London; SAGE.

Rosell-Aguilar, F. (2007). Top of the Pods - In search of a podcasting "podagogy" for language learning. *Computer Assisted Language Learning*, *20*(5), 471–492.

Self, J.A. & Baek, J.S. (2017). Interdisciplinarity in design education: understanding the undergraduate student experience. *International Journal of Technology and Design Education*, 27, 459-480.

Spinelli, M. & Dann, L. (2019). *Podcasting: The Audio Media Revolution*. Bloomsbury.

Thaman, R.G., et al. (2013). Promoting active learning in respiratory physiology – positive student perception and improved outcomes. *National Journal of Physiology, Pharmacy, and Pharmacology, 3*(1), 27-34.

Vogele, C. & Gard, E.T. (2006). Podcasting for corporations and universities: look before you leap. *Journal of Internet Law*, *10*(4), 3-13.

TESSA DIPHOORN, PhD, is an Associate Professor at the Department of Cultural Anthropology, Utrecht University, the Netherlands. Her research and teaching focuses on policing, security, and everyday authority. Email: t.g.diphoorn@uu.nl

BRIANNE MCGONIGLE LEYH, PhD, is Associate Professor of human rights law and global justice. Her research and teaching focuses on conflict and security, international criminal law, transitional justice, victims' rights, and documentation and accountability for serious human rights violations. Email: b.n.mcgonigle@uu.nl

Manuscript submitted: ***May 1, 2022***
Manuscript revised: ***August 23, 2022***
Accepted for publication: ***October 15, 2022***

Peer-Reviewed Article

How Concepts Travel in Actual Spaces: The Interdisciplinary Classroom as a Behavior Setting

Annemarie Kalis
Utrecht University, The Netherlands

ABSTRACT

In interdisciplinary education, students find out that even basic concepts such as time, freedom or control mean different things for different disciplines and individuals. Through such encounters, students develop an ever-richer conceptual toolbox for making sense of the world. But, how do concepts travel (Bal, 2002) in an interdisciplinary classroom? I address this question from the perspective of behavior settings theory, which shows how the concrete spatiotemporal characteristics of an environment structure and guide the behavior of its participants. By means of a case study, I analyze the interdisciplinary classroom as a behavior setting and argue that concepts can travel when the setting stimulates students and teachers to spend time and interact with each other in specific ways.

Keywords: behavior settings, interdisciplinarity, traveling concepts

INTRODUCTION

As outlined in the introduction to this special issue, concepts play a crucial role in interdisciplinary education. In line with the other contributions to this special issue, I use the term concepts to refer to "theoretical tools or "miniature theories" (Bal, 2002, p. 22) that have been developed and used in different disciplinary contexts to name and define themes, problems, and relevant questions" (Diphoorn et al., this issue). What concepts mean is anything but set in stone: their meaning evolves from how they are 'appropriated, translated and kept up to date over and over again and always with a difference' (Neumann & Nünning, 2012, p. 4). Focusing on interdisciplinary research, Bal has argued that their dynamic and fluid character makes concepts, and not methods, the most fruitful 'carrier' of interdisciplinary exchange. However, for this to happen, concepts must *travel* (Bal, 2002). In moving between disciplines and between academics, concepts transform and grow and contribute to interdisciplinary understanding. As Van der Tuin and Verhoeff (2022) propose, concepts could be seen as 'partners in thinking and making' (p. 6). In this special issue, we argue that the traveling of concepts is not only an important tool for interdisciplinary research but also for interdisciplinary education.

In being confronted with people with divergent disciplinary backgrounds, students find out that even basic concepts such as time, freedom, or control actually mean very different things for different disciplines and individuals. Through such encounters, students learn from one another and develop an ever richer conceptual toolbox for making sense of the world. But, how do concepts travel? By taking the metaphor of traveling concepts too literally, one might come to think that concepts move from person to person, from discipline to discipline all by themselves. However, obviously concepts can travel only insofar as people actually make this happen. In this chapter, I argue that for concepts to travel in interdisciplinary education, teachers and students should actually meet for a certain amount of time in a certain kind of shared concrete space. Moreover, I aim to show that to better understand how this works, it is helpful to analyze the interdisciplinary classroom as a behavior setting (Barker, 1968; Pedersen, 2019; Heft, 2020).

The aim of this paper is to examine how concepts travel in a concrete interdisciplinary teaching environment. In the literature review, I first introduce behavior settings theory and show how it has recently been applied in the context of education (Wright et al., 1951; Pedersen & Bang, 2016; Pedersen, 2019). The crucial contribution of behavior settings theory is the insight that both students and teachers experience the concrete teaching environment not "neutrally" but in terms of its affordances or functional, moral and conventional possibilities (Heft, 2018). In the remainder of the paper, I apply behavior settings theory to an exploratory and informal case study by analyzing the concrete teaching environment of Descartes College, the interdisciplinary honors program for bachelor students at Utrecht University, where I am a teacher and program leader. On the basis of classroom observations and exploratory analysis of students' reflection reports and evaluations, I argue that the interdisciplinary classroom of Descartes College can be understood as a behavior setting that both constrains and enables certain forms of behavior. Importantly, the temporal, spatial and social organization of the classroom can both facilitate and hinder the travel of concepts. As I will show, this became especially poignant during the COVID-19 pandemic, when the classroom suddenly needed to be moved to an online behavior setting, with different characteristics and constraints. In the conclusion, I raise the more general question of how one could structure a teaching environment in such a way that it invites the traveling of concepts. I offer some concrete suggestions and map out paths for future exploration in the final section.

In line with the general approach taken in this special issue, what I provide in the article is neither an abstract theoretical analysis nor a full-fledged empirical study. Instead, I report on both the classroom observations I made as a teacher in the program and on written and oral comments received from students in reflection reports and evaluations. By analyzing these observations and students' responses from the perspective of the behavior setting framework, I aim to contribute to a better understanding of how concepts travel in interdisciplinary classrooms.

LITERATURE REVIEW

The notion of behavior setting has its origin in the work of psychologists Roger Barker and Herbert Wright. In the 1960s, they created the Midwest Psychological Field Station, a research station devoted to collecting data about the daily behavior of a group of children living in the village of Oskaloosa, Kansas. During this project, Barker & Wright realized that they "could predict many aspects of children's behavior more adequately from knowledge of the behavior characteristics of the drugstores, arithmetic classes, and basketball games that they inhabited than from knowledge of the behavior tendencies of the particular children" (Barker, 1978, p. 42). Starting from this insight, they developed a framework (influenced by, among others, Kurt Lewin's field theory, see Popov & Chompalov (2012)) that aimed to show how the spatiotemporal characteristics of different environments (a classroom, a drugstore, a library, a baseball game) structure and guide the behavior of the participants in that environment. They define a behavior setting as a space–time ecological unit, or a dynamic, quasistable pattern of "joint activities of two or more individuals that endure for some length of time" (Heft, 2018, p. 109). Their work has given rise to a broader theoretical framework labeled 'behavior settings theory' (Wicker, 1984; Heft, 2001; Popov & Chompalov, 2012), which aims to analyze human behavior by means of a holistic approach. Its main tenet is that to explain what individuals do, one needs to take the whole environmental context (both material and social) into account. The behavior settings framework has not truly become 'mainstream' in psychology, possibly because its main claims deviate from psychology's general focus on explaining the features of individuals and from its commitment to the experimental method (Scott, 2005). Nevertheless, it has given rise to various long-term research programmes in ecological psychology (Perkins et al., 1988; Heft, 2001). Later versions of the approach have made an attempt to show that behavior settings theory should (and can) also take personality factors and subjective experiences of individual agents into account (Wicker, 1984; Fuhrer, 1990).

A core feature of behavior settings is that they are identified in terms of what agents can do and think in them. Thus, to describe a situation as a behavior setting is to describe it in terms of the possibilities that the situation offers to particular individuals. As Harry Heft (2018, 2020) shows, here, Barker & Wright's understanding of behavior settings leans close to the tradition of ecological psychology, which emphasizes that individuals perceive their environment in terms of what it affords doing (Chemero, 2003; Gibson, 1977). In ecological psychology, affordances are understood as relational features: they describe the possibilities for action a certain environment has to offer for creatures with specific features and skills. A book affords reading (next to other actions, such as burning it in a fire) but only for beings that know how to read. Understood in this way, behavior settings offer different affordances to the individuals taking part in them. As Heft (2018) illustrates, "Children in a language lesson most probably would be sitting, reading, listening, writing, speaking when called on to do so, and so on, with these actions supported by the affordances of the classroom. At the same time, the possibility that any individual child would be running, shouting, or tossing a ball is vanishingly small". (p. 108)

This quote points toward an important aspect. Behavior settings not only offer possibilities but also impose normative constraints: "the actions of individuals are appropriate, within a range of normative possibilities, with respect to the place where they occur" (Heft, 2020). The norms imposed in behavior settings can be widely varied in nature. Many of them are conventional, while others are moral (behaviors such as hitting a teacher in the classroom are usually considered morally wrong) or legal (in many places, smoking is legally prohibited). Sometimes the norms at stake are explicit (think of a sign in the classroom listing rules for acceptable behavior), but often they are not. We know that people are not supposed to play loud music or give dinner parties in libraries, even if no one has ever explicitly told us so.

Whereas the framework of analyzing environments as behavior settings is a general one, it has been shown to be especially fruitful for understanding how educational settings contribute to (or hinder) the development of students. This should not come as a surprise, given that the Midwest Psychological Field Station was created with the aim of studying the everyday behavior of children. Both Barker and Wright themselves and later psychologists inspired by their work (such as Heft) provide many specific insights into how classrooms as behavior settings structure children's behavior (Wright et al., 1951; Heft, 2018). Building on this potential, recent work in developmental psychology has brought forward behavior setting theory as a valuable 'ecological' counterpart to more individualist, cognitivist understandings of how children develop, with a specific focus on development in education (Bang, 2012; Pedersen & Bang, 2016; Pedersen, 2019).

What is particularly interesting about these recent contributions is that they show how the norms that guide the behavior of students in a classroom are usually deeply ingrained in its spatiotemporal organization. With regard to temporal organization, many types of classrooms work according to the idea that specific activities happen at specific times in the day and in the week. As such a temporal structure is maintained over an extensive period of time, students come to know what to expect (in a primary school setting, this could be something like 'we do arithmetic before lunch, and after lunch we read and then play outside'). Regarding spatial organization, an obvious feature is the way the teacher and the students are seated in a classroom. However, Bang (2008) also emphasizes the importance of artifacts in providing normative guidance. The presence of books in a classroom suggests that reading is one of the activities that is encouraged, and the absence of fried snacks in the school cafeteria indicates that eating unhealthy food is discouraged.

Of particular relevance for interdisciplinary education is Bang's claim that certain forms of spatiotemporal organization and artifacts offer potential for what she calls developmental novelty. A classroom space that is supportive of development is a space that allows the student "to expand her activities, interact in new ways and/or with new people; and when [she] begins to experience herself and her life in new ways" (p. 163). As an example, Bang describes the presence in some primary school classrooms of carpets "spread out like small 'islands' with a relative freedom from the teacher's control—but only relative, he wants to be able to see them all, probably to be able to help as well as to keep in control" (p. 179). In a similar vein, Pedersen shows that some behavior settings are much more restrictive than others, even in cases where they happen to take place in the same physical space:

"During math class, students sit at their desks all facing the teacher, who is using the whiteboard to go through mathematical proofs. The students take notes on their computers (and some are on Facebook or playing online games!). [...] Then when the bell rings, and recess begins, the same room is immediately used in new ways; new rules and standards apply. This means that people are now sitting on the tables, playing loud music from their computers, shouting, eating, laughing, and playing. Finally, when there is a Friday bar at the school, the classroom often serves as a private room to sneak into, for a private conversation or for a secret kiss. Then the otherwise public room suddenly is perceived as a private place that allows for intimacy" (2019, p. 218).

This example shows that even though behavior settings are partly constituted by a specific physical environment, they cannot be reduced to it. A math class is a math class because it takes place in a certain space, with certain people and artifacts present that all interact with the physical space in specific ways.

In the next sections, I build on the behavior settings framework and the way it has been brought to bear on educational settings in the recent work of Bang and Pedersen. By introducing a concrete case study, I aim to show how the interdisciplinary classroom can be understood as a behavior setting that offers specific possibilities for developmental novelty and, more specifically, how the structure of a behavior setting can either encourage or discourage students from making concepts travel. To offer the necessary background, the next section will provide a general description of the main features of the Descartes College; in the subsequent section, I will proceed to analyze this concrete teaching environment in terms of the behavior setting framework.

THE DESCARTES COLLEGE

The Descartes College is the interdisciplinary honors programme for bachelor students of Utrecht University (The Netherlands). The program aims to enable students from all over the university "to see how your own discipline relates to others" (https://students.uu.nl/en/academics/honours/programs/descartes-college). Students are selected not so much on grounds of past performance but on the basis of a motivation letter where the selection committee specifically looks at their interest in interdisciplinary exchange. It is a two-year program consisting of four courses (each guided by a broad theme) in which students attend weekly guest lectures, organize discussions after the lecture, and work on interdisciplinary assignments, both individually and in small groups. Students enroll in the second year of their usually 3-year bachelor's programme, which means that when they start in Descartes College, they already have some basic disciplinary grounding. What the program offers is a wide range of insights from other academic fields (providing opportunities for perspective taking) and tools for addressing broad questions and problems by collaborating in multidisciplinary teams (helping them to find common ground and achieve integration, see Repko and Szostak (2021)). The Descartes College is an interesting case study for the topic at hand, as various elements of the program can be understood as being directed at the travel of concepts, even when this is usually not explicitly described in these terms. The travel of concepts is stimulated at various levels: both in individual lectures and discussion sessions and on a more abstract level in the development of the final course of the program. To give an example of individual sessions, guest speakers in the program (usually academics from various fields, and sometimes nonacademic experts) often use concepts that do not traditionally belong to their own discipline to explain certain disciplinary ideas. For example, to explain how different kinds of numbers behave differently under mathematical operations, a professor of mathematics stated that 'some numbers can bounce, whereas others cannot'. By giving the concept of bouncing a nonstandard application (to numbers), the teacher made this concept travel. By doing so, he made it possible for students to develop a glimpse of mathematical understanding by nonmathematical means.

After such lectures, student-led discussions often lead to questions for clarification of core concepts of the discipline under discussion. Students are expected to provide statements for discussion, but these often refer to concepts (such as 'equality' or 'force') that are ambivalent and/or have context-dependent meaning. This often leads to questions and comments from the other students, asking them to make hidden assumptions explicit. These discussions frequently reveal the fact that concepts are used differently in different disciplines.

On a more abstract level, the program aims to facilitate the travel of concepts by giving students themselves the responsibility for developing the final course of the program. To structure this course, students should decide on an overarching theme, a concept that should be specific enough to be actually guiding but broad enough to allow for a variety of disciplinary angles. Examples of chosen themes are 'boundaries' (cohort 2017-2019) or 'metamorphosis' (cohort 2018-2020). In preparing this course, the students thus need to let these concepts travel by reflecting on and discussing different possible perspectives on these themes within their group.

At the end of each course, students in Descartes College write an assignment in which they are invited to reflect on their experiences in the program. In addition to these assignments, we regularly hold individual meetings with each student in which we ask their feedback on the course and discuss their interdisciplinary development by asking reflective questions (see Keestra, 2017). In the next section, I will take a closer look at the concrete spatiotemporal and material organization of the classroom of Descartes College and at students' experiences and feedback. I will analyze this material from the perspective of behavior settings theory to clarify the role of the concrete spatiotemporal teaching environment in the traveling of concepts. After that, I will compare this teaching environment with the spatiotemporal and material organization of the classroom during the COVID-19 pandemic.

THE INTERDISCIPLINARY CLASSROOM AS BEHAVIOR SETTING

In this section, I look at the Descartes College as being organized in a specific behavior setting or a closely intertwined duo of behavior settings. As mentioned in the introduction, this exploratory and informal analysis makes use of two kinds of sources: first, I build on my own classroom observations (which took place over a period of five years, 2017-2022) as a teacher in the programme. Second, I use insights provided by students in their reflection assignments and in their evaluations of the programme. By analyzing these personal reports from the perspective of the behavior settings framework, I hope to provide some insight into how concepts travel in this concrete teaching environment.

The core behavior setting that constitutes the Descartes College is the weekly classroom meeting, and this is combined with the informal meeting with pizza and drinks in the university cafeteria afterwards. I analyze these two settings and students' experiences in them first in terms of their temporal structure and then in terms of their spatial and material organization. The most remarkable temporal feature of the way Descartes College is organized is its duration. The program lasts two years, thus spanning two-thirds of students' bachelor's programs. During these two years, they meet on a weekly basis in (usually) the same physical classroom for a lecture, with a discussion session and informal pizza and drinks in the university cafeteria afterwards. In both reflection assignments and evaluations, students indicate that both the duration and continuity of the program play a crucial role in enabling the travel of concepts between students and between teachers and students. For example, in their reflection assignments, several students emphasized that the duration of the program gave them time to determine 'how to get out of their own bubble' and to learn how to engage in critical but also open and unbiased conversations with others that do not share their basic assumptions. The standard duration of regular courses within Utrecht University (usually seven or eight weeks of teaching per course) is in most cases way too short for bringing about such a process. In their second year, several students independently reported that they had come to see their academic environment as a (quite privileged) closed circle and asked for the inclusion of more nonacademic experts in the program to help them obtain a better grasp of societal challenges such as climate change and social inequality. The discussions with such nonacademic speakers that followed also led to novel understandings of concepts such as responsibility, justice and respect: in, for example, 'activist' contexts, such concepts have different connotations than in an academic environment.

Students also report that during their two years in the program, they develop a strong feeling of belonging within the group and explain that in this sense, it is like "being in high school again." Additionally, the extended timespan makes it possible to establish the normative and social structure that constitutes a behavior setting in which expectations and standards are gradually developed. For example, as teachers, we emphasize from the start that it is important that students speak their minds and participate in discussions: such participation plays a crucial role in making concepts travel. However, many students need quite a bit of time before they "get the feel" of the program and feel comfortable and secure enough to participate. Whereas the learning curve of students is steep for some students, it is more gradual for others, and the timespan of two years allows students to develop within the structure of the program according to their own pace. In a traditional seven-week course, there is just not enough time to allow for such diverging developmental trajectories. Another relevant temporal feature is the fact that the weekly lectures and discussions are directly followed by drinks and pizza in the university cafeteria. This temporal order is important because it facilitates students and teachers to follow up and exchange reflections and experiences on the class that just took place.

In addition to these temporal features, the spatial and material organization of both the classroom meetings and the pizza sessions are also structured in a way that encourages the travel of concepts. The class is held in a wide room (approximately 30 feet wide and 13 feet deep) with only four rows of tables, which means that all students (a group has approximately thirty participants) sit relatively close to those who speak at the front. A very simple but powerful artifact is the namebadge. Students acquire a namebadge at the beginning of the program that they put in front of them in every session. In this way, everyone learns each other's names quickly, and guest speakers who join the program for only one session can easily address students by their names.

Additionally, in discussions, students are often encouraged to move around. For example, they must form small groups for discussion or take a certain position in the room while engaging in a debate. Every week, one group of three or four students is responsible for introducing the guest speaker and chairing the discussion, and this requires them to take a different position in the classroom. They need to relocate to the front of the classroom to engage with the guest speaker and to address the group. By enabling students to group and regroup easily within the room, informal and dynamic exchange is stimulated, and students are encouraged to take on different roles with different responsibilities. Especially during the discussion session that follows the lecture, the behavior setting subtly adapts in that now the students are in charge. Thus, the classroom is flipped, enabling active learning (Roehl et al., 2013; Reyna, 2015). In this part of the session, the physical space acquires more degrees of freedom, encouraging an increased level of what Bang (2008) refers to as developmental novelty.

Apart from the classroom sessions, the spatial and material organization of the pizza sessions plays a similar facilitating role. These sessions are held in the university cafeteria housed in the same building, but which forms a very different environment. During the pizza sessions, the cafeteria is not staffed, and the space is reserved more or less exclusively for the students of Descartes College. Students sit at very large rectangular tables, they can take drinks from a cart and share the pizzas that are delivered from a nearby restaurant. This creates a space that is still clearly a university setting but with no supervision and a very high level of freedom. Even though the teachers often join them for a drink, this is not necessarily the case, and the meetings are generally experienced as being first 'for and by' the students. This very informal setting encourages students to exchange their experiences. Many students reported that during discussions over pizza, it is much easier to bring up speculative ideas and questions about the classroom meeting than in the meeting itself. Many students report feeling 'out of their depth' while discussing topics in class that go beyond their disciplinary expertise. Addressing such feelings of uncertainty and vulnerability might be crucial for making concepts travel. Students need to take the leap to let go of their 'disciplinary anchors' to be able to work with concepts from various disciplinary perspectives.

Additionally, the characteristics of the pizza and drinks setting make it easier for students to get to know each other personally and to make friends. Many students reported that their participation in the Descartes College made them grow as persons and as academics and that these changes mostly took place because they got to know and befriend people with views and backgrounds that differed from their own (for the importance of personal relations in interdisciplinary education, see Haynes & Leonard, 2010; Fortuin & Van Koppen, 2016). For example, a group of three students who had to make a podcast together reported that before getting to work, they chatted for hours, had drinks and got to know each other (they did not have many opportunities to meet before due to COVID restrictions). When they met again the next day, making the actual podcast went smoothly. Because they already knew where each of them stood and how they could talk together, making something together was now an easy step to take. As one of them said, 'in order to make something together you first need to get how the other person is thinking' (for similar experiences see Diphoorn & McGonigle Leyh, this issue).

In general, assignments are also structured in a way that encourages students to get together and explore how their perspectives differ and could (or could not) be integrated. Each group of students responsible for that week's discussion is instructed to meet beforehand and develop 1) a format for the discussion and 2) an assignment for all students that has the aim of preparing them for the discussion session. The teachers give feedback on their proposal and encourage students to experiment with different formats and media for organizing the discussions. This is the part of the program students struggle with most. They find it difficult to develop formats for discussion that are original and that contribute to valuable exchange. Especially when they advance propositions for group discussion (propositions such as 'It is wrong to sell one's organs'), these propositions are often criticized by the rest of the group as being ambiguous or impossible to evaluate due to a lack of background information. An example where this led to much debate was a set of propositions brought forward in a discussion about the naturalness or unnaturalness of different forms of sexual behavior. The students that prepared the session had developed propositions such as "it is natural to be sexually attracted to objects." The group found it very difficult and even frustrating to discuss propositions related to this topic because they turned out to have widely divergent understandings of the concept 'natural'. Some took this to mean 'given at birth', whereas others argued that everything that is found in nature can be considered 'natural'. Afterwards, some students concluded that a discussion about a concept without first agreeing on a shared definition is useless; some wrote that talking past each other in this way had been a waste of time. On the other hand, others reported that these disagreements had given them insight into how one's interpretation of a simple word can make a huge difference for how one thinks. While challenging for students, precisely the discovery of such ambiguity and divergence in interpretation seems crucial to the understanding of concepts and whether and how they travel. Even if at points the process is frustrating (see also Leonard, 2012; Augsburg, 2014; Huysmans, this issue), it seems an important step to bring about the kind of experiences students most appreciate in the program: the 'broadening of their horizons' and 'getting out of their bubble'. Even though it is obvious that these kinds of experiences can in principle occur in different settings, the temporal and spatial characteristics of the behavior settings of Descartes College discussed above play an important role in facilitating precisely this kind of exchange.

By applying the behavior settings framework to Descartes College as a case study, I have tried to show how a concrete interdisciplinary classroom is organized in space and in time in such a way that it supports the travel of concepts. In the next section, I will examine what happens if one takes such an interdisciplinary classroom online.

A COMPARISON: THE ONLINE INTERDISCIPLINARY CLASSROOM

In the period March-July 2020, all teaching had to move online due to the COVID-19 pandemic. During this time, the weekly meetings of the Descartes College were held via MS Teams, and even after this period, the meetings were held in a hybrid format. In this way, students or teachers suffering symptoms or quarantine restrictions could attend online, while the rest of the group was present on campus, although in a much bigger room due to social distancing rules. This situation could be seen as a 'forced experiment' that gave much insight into what happens when a behavioral structure is suddenly moved to a fully or partially online setting.

In the regularly held individual meetings with students, it became obvious that almost all students experienced this change as a loss, even if they were grateful that this arrangement allowed the program to be continued during lockdowns. The most important changes students reported were first a decrease in motivation and concentration when listening to an online lecture or participating in an online discussion and second a feeling of being socially isolated from the other students in the program. Meeting online made it more difficult to get to know each other and led to students reporting that they did not truly feel they were part of a group. As one student reported when comparing the online meetings to the meetings on location during his first year in the program, "That what makes the Descartes College unique, the social interaction between students with very different backgrounds, was completely absent in the online classroom". This corresponds to similar observations found in studies on 'regular' online teaching (Kebritchi et al., 2017).

Additionally, students seemed much more reluctant to contribute to a discussion in an online classroom, and as a teacher, I found motivating them much more difficult. In an online environment, it turned out to be almost impossible to bring about the kind of 'frustrating but illuminating' discussions about the meaning of concepts that were described in the previous section. However, the online teaching environment also offered certain advantages: when students discuss in small groups in online breakout rooms, they found it easier to speak up and were not distracted in the way they can be when students work in groups in the same physical classroom (for discussion of advantages and disadvantages of online discussion see Baglione & Nastanski, 2007; Dumford & Miller, 2018).

Whereas these insights are general and hardly systematic, they provide some insight into how online behavior settings change the prospects for concepts to travel in interdisciplinary education. At least some features of the offline behavior setting that are experienced as fundamental (the fact that it invites informal exchange, the physical closeness of people with different perspectives) seem to be lost in the transformation to an online space. As such, it is at least plausible to think that this change has hindered the travel of concepts in Descartes College. This is not to say that it is impossible to design forms of online interdisciplinary teaching that foster the travel of concepts. For example, online spaces enable exchange between people from different backgrounds who live all over the world and thus would never come together in the same classroom. However, when an interdisciplinary program is structured in such a way that being able to move around in the classroom in flexible ways and ample opportunities for informal exchange are crucial features, then a transition of this same structure to an online environment seems to lead to a decrease in valuable exchanges across disciplines.

DISCUSSION AND CONCLUSIONS

In this final section, I take a step back from the Descartes College and raise the general question of how the spaces in which interdisciplinary education takes place could be organized in such a way that they invite the traveling of concepts. Pedersen and Bang (2016) emphasize that behavior settings should certainly not be seen as structures that only constrain or even causally determine the behavior of individuals. As already mentioned in an earlier section of the paper, throughout the history of behavior settings theory, several contributors (most notably Wicker (1984) and Heft (2001), but see also Pedersen (2019)) have emphasized that students and teachers are active and meaning-making individuals who relate to the behavior settings in which they participate in active and not always predictable ways. As the researchers in the Midwest Psychological Field Station reported, "In any setting anything can happen – as a teacher facing a classroom full of children knows well" (Wright et al., 1951, p. 190). The aim of structuring an interdisciplinary teaching environment should thus not be to make students think or act in specific ways but to support and stimulate the development of students' autonomy and competences (see Van der Lecq (2016); for more general arguments on the relation between teaching and autonomy, see Ryle (1971), Bakhurst (2011) and Rödl (2016)). Therefore, what we want to determine is how to structure the relevant behavior settings in such a way that they offer functional and normative possibilities for the traveling of concepts and increase their potential for developmental novelty.

The experiences of students and teachers in Descartes College described above offer suggestions for some concrete features of behavior settings that seem to contribute to this. The first is the temporal aspect: the amount of time spent together seems to be a very important factor. As said, in organizing a two-year program, Descartes College has adopted a highly unusual format in Dutch academic education. As I have tried to show, for traveling concepts, duration is crucial. The normative patterns characterizing behavior settings ('how we do things here') that enable this kind of exchange and development cannot be established overnight. Second, the availability of spatial and material resources for specific forms of exchange also seems to play a crucial role (Chawla & Heft, 2002; Heft, 2018). This can be as simple as using nametags or as using a classroom that allows students to move around, group and regroup in flexible ways. However, even the pizzas could be seen as important artifacts that enable students to talk together, work together and make new friends that broaden their understanding of the world.

These suggestions are mere starting points, and they should not be seen as guidelines but as experiments that have proven their value over time. Room for experimentation might turn out to be the crucial feature of behavior settings that facilitate the travel of concepts. As Bang argues, developmental novelty occurs when the student "begins to experience herself and her life in new ways" (2008, p. 163). However, developmental novelty as a long-term process in the student (which she refers to as 'great novelty') is actually brought about by an extensive pattern of 'small novelties' or everyday experiences in which the student "may find her way in not so well-known surroundings. She may develop new actions, relate to new people or to well-known people in new ways. She may experience herself as a participant in new ways, etc." (p. 163). The challenge thus is to determine how specific settings could invite these kinds of small novelties on an everyday basis. As seen in the section about online teaching, putting students from different backgrounds in the same space does not automatically lead to the travel of concepts. Both the teachers and the students need to make an effort and think creatively on how to bring this about. This means that both teachers and students should have space and time to experiment with the structure of their environment.

To conclude, in this paper, I hope to have contributed to our understanding of how concepts travel in interdisciplinary education. The perspective of behavior settings theory helps to explain how the concrete spatiotemporal characteristics of a classroom structure and guide the behavior of both students and teachers. By describing the behavior settings of Descartes College as a case study, I have tried to show that the interdisciplinary classroom is more than an abstract notion: it is an actual place in which students and teachers spend time, move around and interact with each other and with the objects that surround them. It is in these actual places that concepts travel: not in an ethereal abstract sense, but very concretely—from one student to the next, while they sit at a table and share a slice of pizza.

ACKNOWLEDGEMENTS

This contribution was supported by a research grant from the Dutch Research Council (NWO VI.VIDI.195.116) and by the Utrecht Young Academy. The author would like to thank Miguel Segundo-Ortin, Tessa Diphoorn, Brianne McGonigle Leyh, Martijn Huysmans and two anonymous reviewers for valuable feedback on an earlier version of the manuscript.

REFERENCES

Augsburg, T. (2014). Becoming transdisciplinary: The emergence of the transdisciplinary individual. *World Futures, 70*(3-4), 233-247. http://dx.doi.org/10.1080/02604027.2014.934639

Baglione, S. L., & Nastanski, M. (2007). The superiority of online discussion: Faculty perceptions. *Quarterly Review of Distance Education, 8*(2), 139-150.

Bakhurst, D. (2011). *The formation of reason.* Wiley-Blackwell.

Bal, M. (2002). *Travelling Concepts in the Humanities: A Rough Guide.* University of Toronto Press.

Bang, J. (2012). An environmental affordance perspective on the study of development–artefacts, social others, and self. In *World Yearbook of Education* 2009 (pp. 181–201), Routledge.

Barker, R. G. (1968). *Ecological Psychology: Concepts and methods for studying the environment of human behavior.* Stanford University Press

Barker, R. G. (Ed.). (1978). *Habitats, environments, and human behavior: Studies in ecological psychology and eco-behavioral science from the Midwest Psychological Field Station, 1947 - 1972* (1st ed). Jossey-Bass.

Chawla, L., & Heft, H. (2002). Children's competence and the ecology of communities: a functional approach to the evaluation of participation. *Journal of Environmental Psychology, 22*(1-2), 201-216. http://dx.doi.org/10.1006/jevp.2002.0244

Chemero, A. (2003). An Outline of a Theory of Affordances. *Ecological Psychology, 15*(2), 181–195. https://doi.org/10.1207/S15326969ECO1502_5

Diphoorn, T., Huysmans, M., Knittel, S.C., McGonigle Leyh, B., & Van Goch, M. (under review, this issue). Traveling Concepts in the Classroom: Experiences in Interdisciplinary Education.

Diphoorn, T. & McGonigle Leyh, B. (under review, this issue). Traveling in the Classroom: Podcasting as a Learning Tool for Interdisciplinarity.

Dumford, A. D., & Miller, A. L. (2018). Online learning in higher education: exploring advantages and disadvantages for engagement. *Journal of Computing in Higher Education, 30*(3), 452-465. http://dx.doi.org/10.1007/s12528-018-9179-z

Fortuin, K. P. J., & Van Koppen, C. S. A. (2016). Teaching and learning reflexive skills in inter-and transdisciplinary research: A framework and its application in environmental science education. *Environmental Education Research, 22*(5), 697-716. http://dx.doi.org/10.1080/13504622.2015.1054264

Fuhrer, U. (1990). Bridging the Ecological-Psychological Gap: Behavior Settings as Interfaces. Environment and Behavior, 22(4), 518–537. https://doi.org/10.1177/0013916590224009

Gibson, J. (1977). *The Theory of Affordances. In Perceiving, Acting, and Knowing: Toward an Ecological Psychology.* Lawrence Erlbaum.

Haynes, C., & Leonard, J. B. (2010). From surprise parties to mapmaking: Undergraduate journeys toward interdisciplinary understanding. *The Journal of Higher Education, 81*(5), 645-666. http://dx.doi.org/10.1080/00221546.2010.11779070

Heft, H. (2001). Ecological psychology in context: James Gibson, Roger Barker, and the legacy of William James's radical empiricism. Psychology Press.

Heft, H. (2018). Places: Widening the scope of an ecological approach to perception–action with an emphasis on child development. *Ecological Psychology, 30*(1), 99-123. http://dx.doi.org/10.1080/10407413.2018.1410045

Heft, H. (2020). Ecological psychology as social psychology? *Theory & Psychology, 30*(6), 813-826. http://dx.doi.org/10.1177/0959354320934545

Huysmans, M. (under review). The Market for Kidneys: Bridging Introductory Courses in Economics and Ethics.

Kebritchi, M., Lipschuetz, A., & Santiague, L. (2017). Issues and challenges for teaching successful online courses in higher education: A literature review. *Journal of Educational Technology Systems, 46*(1), 4–29. http://dx.doi.org/10.1177/0047239516661713

Keestra, M. (2017). Metacognition and reflection by interdisciplinary experts: Insights from cognitive science and philosophy. *Issues in Interdisciplinary Studies, 35*, 121-69.

Leonard, J. B. (2012). Integrative Learning: A Grounded Theory. *Issues in Integrative Studies, 30*, 48-74.

Neumann, B. & Nünning A. (2012). Travelling Concepts as a Model for the Study of Culture. In: Neumann, B. & Nünning, A. (Eds.), *Travelling Concepts for the Study of Culture* (pp.1-21). Berlin: De Gruyter. http://dx.doi.org/10.1515/9783110227628.1

Pedersen, S., & Bang, J. (2016). Youth development as Subjectified subjectivity–A dialectical-ecological model of analysis. *Integrative Psychological and Behavioral Science, 50*(3), 470–491. http://dx.doi.org/10.1007/s12124-015-9337-z

Pedersen, S. (2019). Not just a school: Explorations and theoretical considerations in relation to the human eco-niche. In *The 17th Biennial Conference of the International Society for Theoretical Psychology 2017: The Ethos of Theorizing* (pp. 212-221), Captus Press.

Perkins, D. V., Burns, T. F., Perry, J. C., & Nielsen, K. P. (1988). Behavior setting theory and community psychology: An analysis and critique. *Journal of Community Psychology, 16*(4), 355-372. http://dx.doi.org/10.1002/1520-6629(198810)16:4%3C355::AID-JCOP2290160402%3E3.0.CO;2-D

Popov, L., & Chompalov, I. (2012). Crossing over: The interdisciplinary meaning of behavior setting theory. *International Journal of Humanities and Social Science, 2*(19), 18-27.

Repko, A.F. & Szostak, R. (2021). *Interdisciplinary Research: Process and Theory* (4th edition). Sage.

Reyna, J. (2015). Active learning and the flipped classroom. *Training & Development,* October 2015, 30-31.

Rödl, S. (2016). Education and autonomy. *Journal of Philosophy of Education, 50*(1), 84–97. http://dx.doi.org/10.1111/1467-9752.12175

Roehl, A., Reddy, S. L., & Shannon, G. J. (2013). The flipped classroom: An opportunity to engage millennial students through active learning strategies. *Journal of Family & Consumer Sciences, 105*(2), 44-49. http://dx.doi.org/10.14307/JFCS105.2.12

Ryle, G. (1971). Teaching and training. In: *Collected Essays 1929-1968: Collected Papers Volume 2* (pp. 451-64), Hutchinson & Co.

Scott, M. M. (2005). A Powerful Theory and a Paradox: Ecological Psychologists After Barker. *Environment and Behavior, 37*(3), 295–329. https://doi.org/10.1177/0013916504270696

Van der Lecq, R. (2016). Self-Authorship Characteristics of Learners in the Context of an Interdisciplinary Curriculum: Evidence from Reflections. *Issues in Interdisciplinary Studies, 34*, 79-108.

Van der Tuin, I. & Verhoeff, N. (2022) *Critical Concepts for the Creative Humanities*. Rowman & Littlefield.

Wicker, A. W. (1984). *An introduction to ecological psychology.* Cambridge University Press.

Wright, H. F., Barker, R. G., Nall, J., & Schoggen, P. (1951). Toward a psychological ecology of the classroom. *The Journal of Educational Research 45*(3), 187–200. http://dx.doi.org/10.1080/00220671.1951.10881935

ANNEMARIE KALIS, PhD, is an Associate Professor at the Department of Philosophy and Religious Studies, Utrecht University, the Netherlands. Her research and teaching focuses on philosophy of mind, action and cognition. Email: a.kalis@uu.nl

Manuscript submitted: **May 16, 2022**
Manuscript revised: **July 28, 2022**
Accepted for publication: **September 14, 2022**

Peer-Reviewed Article

Scholarly Learning of Teacher-Scholars Engaging in Interdisciplinary Education

Merel van Goch
Institute for Cultural Inquiry, Utrecht University, The Netherlands
Christel Lutz
University College Utrecht, Utrecht University, The Netherlands

ABSTRACT

Many higher education institutions have put interdisciplinary teaching and learning high on their agenda. We know students learn a lot from interdisciplinary education, and we know scholars learn from their educational scholarship, but what do scholars learn from engaging in interdisciplinary *education? I interviewed seven mid-career scholars about what they learned and in what ways their work was appreciated. The findings illustrate that scholars learn about education, students, interdisciplinarity, their own discipline, the university, and themselves, and that the scholars felt their efforts were recognized by their interdisciplinary contexts, but not rewarded outside of those contexts. The study describes academic and personal struggles, pleasures, and joys of scholars starting to engage in interdisciplinary education.*

Keywords: interdisciplinary education, teaching and learning, scholarship, scholarly learning, academic teachers, reflection, interviews

INTRODUCTION

"**D**aunting", "it has the potential to be fun", "a learning experience." When we train academic scholars to teach interdisciplinarity, we invite participants to finish the prompt "Interdisciplinary education is…" These are some of their responses. Scholars' first endeavors in interdisciplinary education are often outside of their comfort zones. But scholars do undertake these activities, because the experience seems promising, and the scholars are curious about what is to come. Indeed, often when we encounter scholars later, they recall enthusiastic anecdotes of what went well, what went wrong, and what they personally and academically got out of the experience. This sparked our curiosity: what happens when scholars start engaging in interdisciplinary education?

It is known that students gain a lot from interdisciplinary education: they excel in critical thinking, meta-cognitive reflection, problem-solving and analysis, and higher order thinking skills (see, for example, Haynes & Brown Leonard, 2010). There is an abundance of literature focusing on the teacher in interdisciplinary education: practical handbooks on how they should teach (e.g., Boor et al., 2021; De Vink et al., 2017) and theoretical works on why that is the case (e.g., Frodeman et al., 2017). We also know that teaching is a learning experience for scholars, as well as interdisciplinarity in itself (Neumann, 2009). Yet what the scholar learns from engaging in interdisciplinary education remains an underexplored research topic. This study therefore explores the research question: what do scholars learn from engaging in interdisciplinary education? We interviewed seven mid-career scholars on what they learned from their first endeavors in interdisciplinary education.

The ones who teach – here, the scholars – should not be overlooked in educational research (Neumann, 2009; Biesta, 2017). The term scholar is used deliberately in this text. There are many ways to refer to the people working in higher education. When focusing on education, they could be called faculty members, teachers, scholars, teacher-scholars, professors, lecturers, staff, or educators. They can be called researchers, scientists, practitioners, or assistant/associate/full professors. These various terms have origins in different areas of focus, disciplines, and geographical locations. Here, we use scholars, to emphasize the full breadth of work in the academe. While their teaching is the motivation for and the focus of this research, we take a broader faculty development perspective on these scholars and regard their work in research and teaching as potentially integrated (Lutz, 2022).

Anna Neumann's (2009) influential work on scholarly learning provides the base of this research (and hence, this article does not focus on professional learning, situated learning, or instrumental learning, even though these are also relevant topics in this context). Neumann interviewed scholars to examine what aspects of their work provided learning for them. Surprisingly – but not surprising perhaps to those who teach (Berg & Seeber, 2018), her participants turned out to learn a lot from teaching: "(…) participating professors associated their scholarly learning with their research activity. Yet a larger number of them related their scholarly learning to their teaching (90% or more)" (p.116). Neumann concludes: "(…) professors' teaching – of graduate and undergraduate students – may be a richer location for their scholarly learning than is their research." (p.118). Interdisciplinarity is mentioned in this work, in relation to research: scholars learned from interdisciplinary research as challenges to habits of mind and due to the novel social interactions (p. 195).

But what about interdisciplinary education? That research and education are related – not only in general, but also in scholars' realities – is described by Ernest Boyer (1990, 1996). He defined four types of scholarship which are related to each other: the scholarship of discovery, the scholarship of integration (i.e., interdisciplinarity), the scholarship of application or engagement, and the scholarship of teaching and learning.

Interdisciplinary education is education in which a complex topic is addressed from the viewpoints of more than one discipline, and/or in which interdisciplinary research is taught (Van Goch, resubmitted; Newell, 2009; Spelt et al., 2009). More and more higher education institutions put interdisciplinary education on their agendas, either developing new interdisciplinary programmes, courses, or lectures, or modifying existing education into more interdisciplinary approaches. As collaborators on other projects on liberal education and on faculty development we agreed on the importance of understanding scholarly learning that happens in the context of interdisciplinary teaching and learning.

Exactly because interdisciplinarity is so ubiquitous in higher education institutions nowadays, it is important to look into what it brings the people who deliver it. This research explores the question: what do scholars learn from engaging in interdisciplinary education? This is a descriptive, exploratory analysis; a first inquiry into this matter. It contributes to our current understanding of scholarly learning, and of interdisciplinary teaching and learning, and thus to the fields of scholarly learning, interdisciplinarity, education and faculty development.

This is the last article in the current special issue on "travelling concepts in interdisciplinary education." Although the focus of this special issue is on travelling concepts (Bal, 2002) in the interdisciplinary classroom, travelling concepts do not take centerstage in this article: the scholars do. Their journeys and experiences working with and reflecting on travelling concepts in interdisciplinary education provided a rich context which allowed us to examine their learning. Our perspectives are that of insiders on the outside. As a scholar of interdisciplinary education (first author) and of faculty development (second author), we share an interest in what students and scholars learn in the context of teaching and learning, and interdisciplinarity is a specific context in which learning seems to be magnified. We have ample experience in interdisciplinarity education, as teachers, researchers and consultants, training individuals and groups. Here, we interviewed our peers to explore what they learned from their first endeavors in interdisciplinary teaching and learning.

METHODOLOGY

Participants

To address our research question, the first author interviewed seven mid-career scholars who were experimenting in interdisciplinary education and reflecting on it in preparation of the current special issue. These scholars participated in a workshop in preparation of this special issue on travelling concepts in interdisciplinary education. Throughout the research process, the first author read their abstracts, drafts, and final articles to re-acquaint herself with their education practices, but these written artefacts were not used for this analysis, since our focus is the scholars' learning, and the focus of the articles is their education practices. Their teaching provided the context, and we were more interested in their own experiences than in the teaching itself. We therefore did not focus on travelling concepts.

The scholars were assistant or associate professors at the time of the interviews. Participants all taught at the same research-intensive university, yet they came from various disciplines: humanities, social sciences, and the natural sciences were all represented. They engaged in different types of interdisciplinary education (sizes ranged from a whole programme or minor, to a course, lecture, or activity) and at different levels (bachelor, master, honours). The reasons for engaging in interdisciplinary education were top-down for some scholars and bottom-up for others: for some scholars it was part of their main duties (e.g., they were hired to develop interdisciplinary education), and for others it was something they did next to their main duties (e.g., they sought funding to design new interdisciplinary education, or they implemented interdisciplinary parts into existing education). Some scholars were compensated for the time they spent on interdisciplinary education (as much as 0.2 fte), others 'did it in their own time', meaning they did it on top of their other work engagements. They self-reported as being 'beginners' in interdisciplinary education, and their experience in interdisciplinary education ranged roughly from 0 years to 5 years.

The scholars did not receive any compensation for their participation in this study. Ethical approval for this project was granted by the ethical committee of the Faculty of Humanities, Utrecht University; all participants gave their consent. Inclusion criteria were merely participation in the making of this special issue. We consider this to be the first exploration of this research topic, which is why it is appropriate that all participants are from the same context; later research could look into the wider context and, for example, compare disciplines, different career stages, or different geographical locations. This study did not set out to do that: we were looking for commonalities, not differences.

Data were collected in the summer of 2021 over the course of three weeks, online via MS Teams. At this moment in time, most interventions had taken place, and the scholars had started writing the chapters. Since we talked about the content of the chapters, which was also the topic of the first author's research, the interviews could be seen as an intervention in themselves, making the scholars aware of their scholarly learning in this situation.

Researcher integrity

This special issue is created by the education committee of the Utrecht Young Academy, a network of early-career scholars interested in academia, policy and society, of which the first author is a member. Members of this committee know each other well. Throughout the research process, the first author reflected on her position as a researcher, and her subjectivity and its influence on the research. Her prior understandings of interdisciplinary education, both as teacher and researcher enhanced the research. Both authors have ample experience with interdisciplinary education, both as teachers and as researchers. We are interested in the topics of scholarly learning and were interested to apply this topic to this sample of people starting to experiment in interdisciplinary education. During the interviews the first author took the role of interviewer, rather than that of expert in interdisciplinary education, and she therefore did not, for example, contradict interviewees. The research was primarily conducted by the first author (design, data collection, analysis, writing), and she consciously reflected on her role during data collection, analysis and the writing phase, using field notes and a research journal. Throughout the research process, the first and second authors discussed the findings, possible codes and themes.

The analysis inherently did include our reflections on certain topics. The findings section of this paper includes excerpts of the data for demonstration purposes. Participants provided feedback on the final paper: they read the final version of this article and gave their approval.

Data collection procedures

Semi-structured interviews were used as a method (Braun & Clarke, 2013), because this was designed to be a descriptive, exploratory study. Ensuring that everyone got asked the same questions enabled us to get a good grasp on the matter. The data collection protocol was developed based on our own experience (which

questions generate elaborate, reflective answers) and on the literature on scholarly learning. The order in which the questions were asked was roughly the same for every interview:
- Why did you develop this intervention?
- How different is this from what you normally do?
- What have you learned about education?
- What have you learned about students?
- What have you learned about interdisciplinarity?
- What have you learned about your discipline?
- What have you learned about the university?
- What have you learned about yourself?
- Do you feel like your efforts are recognized and/or rewarded?
- What surprised you? What would you have liked to know before?
- Is there anything else you would like to discuss?

Before the interviews the first author re-read the abstracts of the articles that the scholars wrote for the current special issue, but these were not used as data. Interviews took 45 minutes to one hour on average; they were recorded on audio and then transcribed.

Analysis

We used a reflexive thematic analysis approach to identify patterns of meaning in the experiences of the scholars. The process of analysis was guided by the thematic analysis phases of Braun and Clarke (2006, 2013, 2021). In all stages, the first and second authors discussed the findings, possible codes and themes, moving back and forth between the six analysis phases.

The first author familiarized herself with the data by immersion (reading the transcriptions and field notes over and over) and critically engaged with the data. Before the analysis she read the drafts of the articles, to re-familiarize herself with the interventions. Throughout this phase she kept adding to her research journal. When she felt she had a good grasp of the data, she moved to the next phase, of data coding, using NVivo. The study's aims were explorative and most of the initial codes were quite semantic. The approach was mostly inductive; she did not work with pre-set codes, but rather the codes were identified in the data. Sometimes codes were deductive, for example when participants mentioned certain didactical or pedagogical strategies. Most codes were semantic, some were latent. Units of analysis differed in size: some were sentences, phrases, words. She also wrote topic summaries per question. This was helpful to immerse herself even more in the data. She then identified themes, and decided to keep the division between interview topics, because of the exploratory nature of this study. She then developed candidate and final themes, staying close to the data.

When we felt comfortable with the final themes, we moved forward to the writing stage. At this point the scholars had finalized their articles, which we re-read and compared to our analysis of our interviews. During the writing stage, the first author presented this work at two conferences, for different audiences, which helped us reflect on the data, the study and its aims even more. We realized that these data can be useful for different audiences and thus can be analyzed in different ways, with different foci. We decided to stay close to the initial idea of focusing on the scholars and their learning, and, for example, not generating recommendations for faculty developers and higher education institutions for now.

FINDINGS

This section presents the findings on what scholars learn from engaging in interdisciplinary education, generated by interviews. The findings are arranged according to topic (learning about education, students, interdisciplinarity, their own discipline, the university, themselves, and recognition) and are illustrated by direct quotes or paraphrases from the interview data.

What the scholars learned about education

What the scholars learned about education can be divided into two themes: *the need for other didactical and pedagogical approaches* and *the role of teaching in scholarship*. Scholars said they had experienced that interdisciplinary education calls for other didactical and pedagogical approaches than what they previously had been doing, as well as how interdisciplinary teaching and learning differs from that within one discipline. This ranged from specific examples such as teaching activities ("activate a frame of reference before you do anything else") and evaluation ("evaluate as soon as possible and be honest about it, be open to improvement."), to more general insights such as: "Create a safe, excited, enthusiastic atmosphere. Trust in the excitement of the encounter. Plan for spontaneity."

Their experiences in interdisciplinary education made the scholars reflect on the role of teaching in their scholarship. For example, one scholar said:

> Interdisciplinary education encourages you to relate your work to other courses and disciplines, to make bridges. You should look at other syllabi in an active manner. Talk to colleagues. It's very informative to see colleagues teach. Monodisciplinary education would also benefit from this, but there is less reason to do this there.

Another scholar discovered the interdisciplinary in their own, disciplinary teaching. They regarded their teaching as monodisciplinary, but by gaining more experience in interdisciplinarity, they discovered that their discipline is more broad than they previously thought.

One of the scholars reflected deeply on the impact teaching can have on scholars:

> Teaching is always a place of anxiety, a place of putting yourself in a vulnerable position. Because you never know when a student in class will actually know more or know different or understand better or whatever than you, which is actually nice, speaks to the intelligence of our students. But when you do this interdisciplinary teaching, there's also the cultural component.

'Cultural', here, was synonym for different disciplines, or fields or cultures within the university or academia. This scholar felt very strongly that this should not be merely the responsibility of the scholar themselves:

> If we want interdisciplinary education to succeed between fields distant from each other, we need to address this aspect of training and personal development of teachers in higher education.

What the scholars learned about students

What their experiences teaching in interdisciplinary education taught scholars about students can be roughly divided into three themes: *a broader view of the student body*, *recalibrating the role of the teacher*, and *the right time and place for interdisciplinarity*. Scholars encountered a variety of students in their interdisciplinary teaching environments, which changed their views of the student body. As one scholar put it: "There is not just one higher education student. There are several."

The broader view of the student body made scholars reflect on the students they had taught before, in their disciplinary teaching. One scholar now "discovered there are fun students and that [they] like working with them." With the word 'fun', they meant: "curious, skilled, ambitious, smart, creative, tenacious students, with perseverance, a lot of brainpower, the ability to have a helicopter view, and who are abstract and conceptual thinkers." This scholar had not encountered these kinds of students before, even though they had been teaching for a long time.

Regarding recalibrating the role of the teacher, scholars reflected on how they had been teaching before, and how their interdisciplinary experiences differed from that, and how this influenced each other: "Students can do way more than you think. You don't have to micromanage them. This is also relevant for my disciplinary education; I'll give them more ownership there too." This scholar was surprised to find that they underestimated their interdisciplinary *and* disciplinary students.

Scholars also reflected on the right time and place for interdisciplinarity: "Interdisciplinarity may not be for everyone. You need basic knowledge about what disciplines are and what your discipline is before you can understand and apply interdisciplinary lenses." This scholar advocated for giving students the chance to grow a solid base in their discipline, as well as a grasp of disciplines in general, before introducing them to interdisciplinarity. Another scholar acknowledged that there may not be one suitable moment for the whole group: "For the majority it's not going to be life-changing. I do it for the one student who will have an aha-moment. That's what it's about."

What the scholars learned about interdisciplinarity

When it comes to what scholars learned about interdisciplinarity, identified themes were: *time and effort, conditions for interdisciplinarity,* and *affect and emotion.* Some scholars talked about interdisciplinarity in general, including transfer from teaching to other parts of scholarship – one scholar exclaimed enthusiastically that engaging in interdisciplinary education "opened [their] view to consider interdisciplinarity in [their] research." Others solely talked about interdisciplinarity teaching and learning. Scholars acknowledged that interdisciplinarity is difficult and takes time, both for the teachers as well as the students. This mostly has to do with the collaborative work: taking the time to get to know each other and each other's perspectives, in each step of the interdisciplinary process. For teachers, this adds up to not only extra time for preparation, but also during the teaching itself, and later during assessment and evaluation. One scholar said quite frankly: "If everybody is understaffed and overworked you cannot do interdisciplinarity." They were worried that higher education institutions' focus on interdisciplinarity would be detrimental to their employees. They continued:

> I understand better why people in my field don't do interdisciplinary work. I can see why they don't, because I can see the difficulty and I can see also that it doesn't necessarily lead anywhere sometimes. But I think they should do more of that. It is important and humbling.

Many scholars acknowledge that engaging in interdisciplinary education costs more time than disciplinary education, particularly in terms of preparation. They lamented the lack of compensation for this increased time and effort.

> The university should acknowledge that interdisciplinarity costs more time; you should get more time to development interdisciplinary education, to go to a Special Interest Group, to develop a network, to talk to each other and read the literature, or do a course. There should be a scenario or protocol for interdisciplinary education to facilitate it. I know there are possibilities, but they don't match our reality in terms of time.

Scholars stressed the significance of support (formal and informal) and facilitation. Some said they felt like they were the only ones 'doing this:' discovering how to approach interdisciplinary education, without proper support, even though they knew that shouldn't be the case. Even scholars who have received money from the university's incentive fund for interdisciplinary teaching thought so. For example, one of them predicted that their project would be short lived, because the incentive fund only covered the first iteration of the newly developed course.

Scholars also talked about the conditions for interdisciplinarity, and they showed interesting contrasts. One scholar said: "An essential ingredient is that you have to respect each other. It takes time, and maybe even being forced to collaborate in an assignment." However, another scholar said: "You can't force it, it's a coalition of the willing. If the willingness is there, the opportunities are infinite." Interestingly, both these scholars considered 'respect' to be an important factor in this regard.

Relatedly, affect and emotion were omnipresent in the answers to this question. Much like the scholar who reflected on the anxiety in interdisciplinary teaching, scholars brought emotions and feelings into the discussion, both positive and negative. One scholar revisited a crucial moment in a co-teaching partnership:

> It can seem really easy. And then at a certain point, and that can be sooner or later, and for us, it was actually relatively late, you realize, oh my, we are talking about vastly different things and we're coming from vastly different traditions and ideas about knowledge and science. You feel the ground opening below you. It's so deceptive. It takes a lot of trust and openness to be able to let it sit. It's okay. It's not about convincing the other person, it's about letting it sit. I think it's very important to have these moments and then to also recover from them. Only then are you actually doing the work, because before you are doing it based on a seeming understanding rather than an actual understanding.

They had been collaborating for a number of years, when they both realized they did not assign similar meanings to a central concept. The scholar said that after that moment:

> (…), our teaching has maybe lost some of the initial excitement, that's normal in any relationship, but it has gained a deeper meaning. The sessions are better because now we really know what we're doing and why it's important.

This scholar likened the co-teaching relationship to any other relationship, including ups and downs and different transformative moments in the relationship.

What the scholars learned about their own discipline

Engaging in interdisciplinary education brought scholars an *introspective view of their discipline*, as well as an *outsider-perspective*. One scholar found out their discipline is actually more interdisciplinary than they thought, but many other scholars observed that their discipline, or their work in general, is more restricted than they thought. One scholar phrased it as follows:

> I am way deeper in my own discipline than I thought. I thought what I did resonated with lots of things, but actually I am hyper specialized and in my own bubble of my own students with our own vocabulary.

Although this realization came from a teaching experience, this scholar also related it to their research:

> It's dangerous, that you're into your own discipline so deep. You need to realize this if you want to collaborate [with other disciplines]. This disciplinary grounding really took place for me. I dare to ask questions about other disciplines now. You are allowed to admit there is a lot you don't know.

Teaching interdisciplinarily also made scholars reflect on how others view their discipline. This was not an easy realization. One scholar said:

> I learned that my discipline is a niche population, also in terms of students. Of course I knew students in my discipline have a bad reputation but now that I saw them together with students from other disciplines, I realized: oh yeah, exactly, there's a truth to it. I knew we were in a bubble, but now I know what it looks like from the outside.

And another scholar reflected:

> What I learned, and that was rather painful and shocking, was that my discipline is always critical. And that's taken as criticism and being a party pooper. I get very upset about it. We're the ones who spoil the fun.

The outsider-perspective on their own discipline was thus very insightful for the scholars.

What the scholars learned about the university

Scholars' experiences in interdisciplinary education also led to learning about the university. The most important themes were *collaboration* and *university politics*. In their answers, some scholars mainly focused on what they learned about the university as an institution in general; others focused on the specific university they are most familiar with. Many scholars elaborated on the difficulty of collaboration across faculties: "It is so important to talk to people outside of your discipline without having a clear goal, and to have a network. But it's difficult to find them." Scholars stressed the necessity of meeting people from outside your building, department or discipline, because it enriches teaching and research experiences, and life in academia in general. The lack of infrastructure (e.g., every discipline in its own building) leads to a lack of opportunities for serendipitous encounters.

Many of the scholars mentioned the importance of networks – formal or informal, top-down or bottom-up – such as the Young Academy all scholars were associated with. Such networks provide the time and space for encounters outside your own building, department or discipline. The scholars stressed that these networks should ideally not be restricted to certain members of the academic community, to prevent gatekeeping and to offer everyone who wants to join the possibility to join.

University politics were also discussed a lot in response to the question what scholars learned about the university. Micromanagement and bureaucracy, for example, were mentioned as hampering innovation in education in general and interdisciplinary education in particular: "A lot is possible if you don't micromanage at the administrative level. There are little villages inside the university where you can do fun stuff without bureaucracy." This scholar did not think these 'little villages' where innovation is thriving will exist for much longer: "…they're vulnerable. I know that's what the university is like, you cannot escape that, but it was nice while it lasted."

Other scholars also mentioned that although incentives such as seed money or incentive funds are nice in the short run, the longer term prospects are not clear. Indeed, money was also an important topic of relevance here:

> The structure of our university is not conducive to collaboration, because people in the humanities are paid less per hour than people in the natural sciences, so I'm losing money if I'm teaching to the humanities. I do it in my own time.

What the scholar means with "I do it in my own time," is that they do not include their interdisciplinary teaching as part of their teaching duties. Several other scholars also indicated, as discussed in the section on what they learned about interdisciplinarity, that – in their experience – interdisciplinary education costs more time than disciplinary education, particularly in terms of preparation. This preparation is done in scholars 'own time', at night, or on the weekends. Some scholars said they were happy to do that because it was worth the effort, although some struggled with the workload.

Another important topic was the university's standpoint on interdisciplinarity versus disciplinarity. One scholar said: "Even though the university says we are multidisciplinary, there is still more appreciation for disciplinary research work. I'm on the tenure track and I have to prioritize disciplinary work." Although this particular university puts interdisciplinarity high on their agenda, the individual scholar does not 'feel' this in their day to day life. Indeed, another scholar remarks:

> The university should acknowledge that interdisciplinarity and disciplinarity can and should exist in parallel. They should acknowledge that not everyone wants to do interdisciplinarity. Or doesn't have the competences. And that's okay! The university doesn't have to choose and can be good in both.

These statements show that the scholars value both disciplinarity and interdisciplinarity, and acknowledge that both have pros and cons. They would like to see this reflected in the university's strategic vision.

What the scholars learned about themselves

When asked what the scholars have learned about themselves, through engaging in interdisciplinary education, most scholars indicated it was a difficult question. A broad range of answers followed, from insights on *(inter)disciplinarity* to *knowledge and learning* in general.

With respect to (inter)disciplinarity, the general gist was that scholars learned that they had a broader interest than they thought, or would like to know more about other disciplines. One scholar said: "I learned that I shouldn't cancel disciplines too soon. I rediscovered my curiosity for other disciplines." This scholar admitted that they were hyper focused on their own discipline and would like to change this in the future. Others didn't just reflect on their current occupation, but went back further in time: "I've learned that I should have chosen a different discipline in high school." This scholar was discouraged to follow their passion for a particular field of science during high school, and now, after teaching students in this field, regrets this choice. They are advocating for better education and information on different disciplines earlier on in childrens' school careers.

Scholars reflected on whether they can 'do' interdisciplinarity. One scholar reflected: "I learned that I can do this kind of stuff, but not with everybody." They acknowledged that they initially found interdisciplinarity intimidating, but learned that with the right people it could work. Another scholar said: "I learned that I can and cannot do it. Sometimes I succeed and sometimes I fail miserably. I cannot estimate this well. And that's fine. I'm learning." They said they usually can predict quite adequately whether a lecture is going to go well, or how to react to certain situations in class, but in interdisciplinary contexts they have a hard time making this judgment.

Scholars said they learned a lot from their students, both in terms of content, as well as about disciplines and fields of science. One scholar said: "I learned that I know a lot about very little. It has broadened my horizon." Another scholar related this learning to job satisfaction and joy: "I enjoy broad learning. This is how you can keep learning. It keeps your job fun." They rediscovered that broad learning stimulates them. One scholar summed it up as follows:

> Even though it's challenging and it's not rewarded, I would do it all over again. It's been one of the nicest, most enriching experiences that I've had. I learned a lot about teaching, about working with colleagues, working with people from different areas. I wish everybody would try it once.

Whether the scholars feel like their efforts are recognized and/or rewarded

The answers to my question on whether the scholars felt like their efforts in interdisciplinary education are recognized and/or rewarded, can be summarized as an overwhelming 'no.' This was an emotional topic for many scholars. In general, the *discrepancy in recognition* between the higher university level, and the grassroots level, or the level of the work floor, is evident in the answers. "Within the interdisciplinary bubble it's extremely appreciated, because everyone knows the value and what it takes. But they are not my manager," said one scholar.

They recognized the difference between appreciation from like-minded peers, students and others who have experience with interdisciplinarity (in research or education), and their direct supervisors or managers. Although this external appreciation is nice, of course, it is in stark contrast with appreciation from the people who actually assess these scholars: "My manager doesn't understand. He is not trained to see or appreciate it. It's new." The middle management layer, thus, seems to not see the need for interdisciplinarity and keeps assessing scholars on older views. This is remarkable since interdisciplinarity plays such an important role in the university's vision. Indeed, the top level of the university does seem to appreciate it, and examples of these scholars' interdisciplinary education receive appreciation on the institute's social media. But it does not correspond with new efforts in recognition, reward and assessment of employees. The scholars interviewed here do not seem to experience the realization of these plans yet:

> The university thinks multidisciplinarity is the norm but it's not. There are many people who do not like interdisciplinarity, who do not value it and who do not appreciate it. And they are assessing us.

For most scholars, their interdisciplinary work is not discussed at the yearly assessment and development meetings, sometimes because the manager does not know about the work, or does not think it is important; sometimes because the employee does not want to draw attention to it because they know it will not be appreciated. This lack of appreciation has severe negative consequences: from denied access to leadership courses and promotions, to lower job satisfaction:

> What this [lack of appreciation] does in the end is that I've also decided for myself that I'm going to allocate more time to research and less to teaching. So I'm not going to do as much of the things that I can do very well and that I like. Because if you won't promote me based on these things, then, well, then I'm going to do less of them, and I'm going to do more of something else. So that defeats the purpose.

This scholar enjoy their interdisciplinary work immensely, they gain a lot of job satisfaction from it, but they have experienced that they will not be promoted if they do not focus more on disciplinary work. So their conclusion is that they will have to stop doing things they enjoy and do well, for the sake of promotion, even though the university says these incentives should not be there anymore.

What surprised the scholars

One of my last questions to the scholars was whether there was something that surprised them. Was there anything they would have wanted to have known before they started their experiments in interdisciplinary education? I asked this question to see if there was anything left undiscussed. In general, the reactions to this question mirrored reactions to other questions, which showed me that we had covered the most important points. Scholars mentioned personal insights, time investment, university politics, and that some aspects of the interdisciplinary teaching and learning were harder and others were easier than expected.

Some scholars reflected on my question on a meta level. One scholar mentioned the limits of interdisciplinarity:

> What I learned and what surprised me is that you can go so far with this and then at a certain point with people from a vastly different discipline, there is a point at which it stops. I guess that's just how it is and how it has to be. Ultimately it shouldn't have surprised me. But it did.

Again, this shows an emotional reaction to the experience of interdisciplinarity. Another scholar answered:

> The pleasure is in the discovery. It's an emergent process. It is nice that you don't know what's going to happen beforehand. I wouldn't have wanted to know a lot beforehand. That would be too goal-directed and utilitarian.

I ended the interviews asking whether we had covered everything the scholar wanted to discuss about these topics, or whether there were any things they wanted to add. The majority of scholars then again stressed the necessity of formal and informal networks for these kind of efforts, for various reasons. Some scholars would not have met the person they were co-teaching with without the Young Academy network they were involved in; others would not have become enthusiastic about interdisciplinarity without hearing about other people's work. These networks are identified as incubation centers for innovation, and the scholars thought their value is immense.

DISCUSSION, IMPLICATIONS, AND CONCLUSIONS

The current study has looked into what scholars learn from engaging in interdisciplinary education. It shows that scholars learn from these endeavors in numerous ways. It also, importantly, shows that scholars do not feel recognized or rewarded for their efforts beyond their immediate contexts of peers, direct colleagues, and students, despite the university's efforts to improve recognition and reward structures. The pleasure and joy, both academically and personally, of the scholars' interdisciplinary work are clear, and so are their struggles.

Scholarly learning

This study again demonstrated Neumann's conclusion that learning doesn't stop at some point in scholars' academic career (Neumann, 2009). This cannot be repeated often enough. The scholars' experiences in interdisciplinary education, and the influence of these new experience to their disciplinary educational practices, resemble Neumann's (2009) observations about her participants' experience in interdisciplinary research:

> Some professors position themselves to learn outside their disciplinary or field-based communities of practice. This need not mean leaving one's home field "for good." Usually, professors who cross into disciplines and fields that are new to them pursue the new knowledge while remaining anchored in their own. Thus, their "trips out" serve as opportunities to "recontextualize" their learning agendas – to view their continuing topics of study in different ways and in different settings – thereby enlarging their understanding of them. (p. 106)

The mid-career scholars in this study were interviewed in relation to their experiences in interdisciplinary education, but our conversations were not limited to education at all. They mentioned research, for example, and the bilateral relationship between research and education. This corresponds with Neumann's findings that scholars' learning from education seeds into other aspects of scholarship, such as research (Neumann, 2009). Of course, this also relates to Boyer's model of scholarship: a scholar does not just do one trick, but engages in many different forms of scholarship at once (Boyer, 1990, 1996). Crossing boundaries from one type of scholarship to another, or from one type of education to another, thus has the potential to be a learning experience (Akkerman & Bakker, 2011; Bronkhorst et al, 2013). As Diphoorn & McGonigle Leyh write, "actively experimenting (…) around interdisciplinarity, has made us better scholars and educators" (this issue).

Interdisciplinary education

With respect to the topic of interdisciplinarity, scholars – through engaging in interdisciplinary education – also learned about their own discipline, and about how various disciplines can differ or overlap. They also reflected meaningfully on their own role in or in-between disciplines. These findings also mirror Neumann's findings on scholars working across disciplinary boundaries (Neumann, 2009), whose participants also valued the outside-in view interdisciplinarity causes. This increased disciplinary self-reflection will benefit not only scholars' disciplinary work, but also their interdisciplinarity, as "good interdisciplinary work requires a strong degree of epistemological self-reflexivity" (Klein, 1996; in Repko & Szostak, 2017).

The analysis also showed that the discrepancy between the loud and soft voices of interdisciplinarity still persists (Lindvig, 2017; Lyall, 2019). This discrepancy, coined by Lindvig (2017), contrasts "the 'loud and performative voice' of interdisciplinarity that is present at strategic, institutional levels with the 'quiet and productive voice' of those engaged in its daily practice" (Lyall, 2019). The paradoxes at play, described in depth by Lindvig and Lyall, are again evident in the realities of the scholars interviewed in this study. The middle management layer, in between the soft and the loud voices, hampers recognition and reward for interdisciplinary efforts, and even, as evidenced by some scholars' necessary move away from interdisciplinarity to meet disciplinary requirements, are hampering interdisciplinarity in general, despite university's strategic plans to promote interdisciplinarity. Indeed, these scholars also face challenges regarding the value and recognition of interdisciplinarity for their career (Lyall, 2019). This mirrors work showing that interdisciplinary "expertise is often neither properly recognized and reward nor appropriately evaluated or assessed" (Hendren and Ku, 2019; Lyall, 2019; Bammer et al., 2020, in Hoffmann et al., 2022).

The scholars' call for support and facilitation of interdisciplinary education is interesting in this matter. The university where they work actually does have multiple structures in place to support and facilitate interdisciplinary teaching and learning. Why don't these structures reach the scholars, and/or why don't the scholars use these structures? This seems to be a similar situation as Lindvig's observation about the academic literature on interdisciplinary education: "In order to find it, you need to know it exists." (Lindvig & Ulriksen, 2019). Institutionalizing interdisciplinarity is a complex matter (Baptista & Klein, 2022), and this is one part of it.

An important additional issue is the question of what is so special about interdisciplinary education. If this study would have been about scholars experimenting in disciplinary education, or maybe those teaching in higher education for the first time, what would the findings have looked like then? Some of the findings would likely have been similar, others are specific to interdisciplinarity. As Lindvig & Ulriksen (2019) state, we should be wary of attributing certain things to interdisciplinarity that are in fact due to other reasons, but obscured because of the black box of interdisciplinarity (Mansilla, 2005).

Reflection and metacognition

By reflecting on and writing about their interdisciplinary education in their own articles (this issue), the scholars were developing their Scholarship of Teaching and Learning (Boyer, 1990, 1996). In their reflections on their experiences in interdisciplinary education and what they learned, the scholars show epistemological fluency (Markauskaite & Goodyear, 2017) and metacognitive awareness (Flavel, 1976; Hartman, 1998; Weiner, 1987).

These interviews could be seen as a light form of reflection-on-action (Schon, 1983), a small intervention in scholars' practice (Ibarra & Barbulescu, 2010). Informal conversations have been shown to be helpful in learning processes of scholars (Thomson & Trigwell, 2018). Regular systematic reflection on their work, and what it means to them, can bring ample benefits to scholars' academic and personal lives (Lutz, Van Goch, & Baker, 2021; Lutz, Untaru, & Van Goch, 2021; Beer, Rodriguez, Taylor, Martinez-Jones, Griffin, Smith, & Anaya, 2015; Greenberger, 2020; Lin et al., 2018; Neumann, 2009; Rodgers, 2002; Schon, 1983), as "reflection is a key part of any active learning" (Diphoorn & McGonigle Leyh, this issue).

Motivation and emotion

None of the conversations in this study focused on constructive alignment, intended learning outcomes, and other terms that are so common in higher education administration and research. Of course, the interview questions were not explicitly aimed to generate such answers – we did not ask how the scholars designed their education, for example, but focused on what they experienced – but it was remarkable that such topics just did not come up.

This indicated to us that the scholars were indeed experimenting, were teaching and learning from the bottom-up, with intrinsic motivation. As stated in the introduction to this special issue (Diphoorn et al., this issue): the scholars stepped outside of their comfort zone. They jumped, and they encountered highs and lows, and they learned, and it brought them joy. They learned by doing (Diphoorn & McGonigle Leyh, this issue). In our conversations they radiated a contagious passion, enthusiasm, and curiosity – even when they were discussing serious matters and negative experiences. One scholar, for example, exclaimed their interdisciplinary teaching collaboration brought them so much joy after the solitude of the covid lockdowns. Some said the collaborations gave them a sense of belonging. But there was also frustration, as can also be read in other works in this issue (Huysmans, this issue; Kalis, this issue) – which once again shows that "students and teacher don't experience the teaching environment as neutral" (Kalis, this issue). Indeed, these experiences – positive and negative – seem to be valuable for scholars' academic and personal lives (Berg & Seeber, 2018; Bronkhorst et al., 2013; Meijer, 2011).

Further research

We deliberately chose to interview a small group of scholars who, although diverse in discipline, are relatively homogeneous, since all scholars were employed as assistant or associate professor at the same research-intensive university. We will not claim, therefore, that this analysis can be generalized to all mid-career scholars, even in the Netherlands. It does seem, though, that these results are in line with a growing body of academic and grey literature on interdisciplinarity and the value and recognition of careers (e.g., Lyall, 2019), and the call for supporting mid-career scholars (Baker et al., 2017; Lutz, 2022).

The goal of this interview study was to gain an overview of what scholars learn from engaging in interdisciplinary education, to identify broad themes worthy of further exploration. This work identified many themes that provide ideas for further research. One valuable line of research could delve deeper into scholars' learning. How can scholars make this self-reflection productive? How would other academic demographics respond to these questions? Are there differences between scholars with more or less teaching experience, or between different disciplines? Future research could also look into how interdisciplinary education unsettles scholars' routine expertise, and whether deliberate practice with this new type of teaching and learning may foster their adaptive expertise (Grunefeld et al., 2022). And what do scholars learn from engaging in interdisciplinary research? How, exactly, does interdisciplinary experience feed into disciplinary work?

On the institutional level also many follow-up questions arise: why do infrastructures and incentives not reach these scholars, even though they have high institutional knowledge, as evidenced by their active participation in university life? Such follow-up work could mirror Lindvig & Ulriksen's (2019) question: if a faculty member from any given discipline, with no prior experience in interdisciplinary teaching, is planning an interdisciplinary course, what institutionally available support and facilitation can they find and use? In the time between the interviews were held and finalizing this manuscript, the university has made the interdisciplinary support and infrastructure even more explicit, including the launch of a university-wide interdisciplinary teaching programme aimed at scholars starting out with interdisciplinarity education. Future research could look into the effects of such explicit efforts. And what can be done about the ongoing divide between the loud and soft voices of interdisciplinarity, especially regarding the middle layer who assesses early career researchers? Preliminary work on how department heads, deans and rectors talk about interdisciplinarity shows high variance and identifies fascinating follow-up questions (Kurtti, 2022).

To conclude, the current study showed that scholars' first experiences with interdisciplinary education provided them with many learning opportunities, personally as well as academically. Interdisciplinary teaching and learning is indeed daunting, fun, as well as a true learning experience.

REFERENCES

Baker, V. L., Terosky, A. L., & Martinez, E. (2017). *Faculty Members' Scholarly Learning Across Institutional Types: ASHE Higher Education Report*. John Wiley & Sons.

Bal, M. (2002). *Travelling concepts in the humanities: A rough guide*. University of Toronto press.

Bammer, G., O'Rourke, M., O'Connell, D., Neuhauser, L., Midgley, G., Klein, J. T., ... & Richardson, G. P. (2020). Expertise in research integration and implementation for tackling complex problems: when is it needed, where can it be found and how can it be strengthened? *Palgrave Communications, 6*(1), 1-16.

Baptista, B. V., & Klein, J. T. (Eds.). (2022). *Institutionalizing interdisciplinarity and transdisciplinarity: collaboration across cultures and communities*. Routledge.

Beer, L. E., Rodriguez, K., Taylor, C., Martinez-Jones, N., Griffin, J., Smith, T. R., ... & Anaya, R. (2015). Awareness, integration and interconnectedness: Contemplative practices of higher education professionals. *Journal of transformative education, 13*(2), 161-185.

Berg, M., & Seeber, B. K. (2018). *The Slow Professor*. University of Toronto Press.

Biesta, G. J. (2017). *The rediscovery of teaching*. Routledge.

Boor, I., Gerritsen, D., de Greef, L., & Rodermans, J. (2021). *Meaningful Assessment in Interdisciplinary Education: A Practical Handbook for University Teachers*. Amsterdam University Press.

Boyer, E. L. (1990). *Scholarship reconsidered: Priorities of the professoriate*. Princeton University Press.

Boyer, E. L. (1996). From scholarship reconsidered to scholarship assessed. *Quest, 48*(2), 129-139.

Braun, V., & Clarke, V. (2006). Using thematic analysis in psychology. *Qualitative research in psychology, 3*(2), 77-101.

Braun, V., & Clarke, V. (2013). *Successful qualitative research: A practical guide for beginners*. SAGE.

Braun, V., & Clarke, V. (2022). *Thematic analysis: A practical guide*. SAGE.

Bronkhorst, L. H., van Rijswijk, M. M., Meijer, P. C., Köster, B., & Vermunt, J. D. (2013). University teachers' collateral transitions: continuity and discontinuity between research and teaching. *Infancia y Aprendizaje, 36*(3), 293-308.

Diphoorn, T., Huysmans, M., Knittel, S.C., McGonigle Leyh, B., & Van Goch, M. (2023). Travelling Concepts in the Classroom: Experiences in Interdisciplinary Education. *Journal of Interdisciplinary Studies in Education*.

Diphoorn, T. & McGonigle Leyh, B. (2023). Travelling in the Classroom: Podcasting as a Learning Tool for Interdisciplinarity. *Journal of Interdisciplinary Studies in Education.*

Flavell, J.H. (1976). *Metacognitive aspects of problem solving*. In L. Resnick, ed., The Nature of Intelligence. Hillsdale, NJ: Lawrence Erlbaum Associates.

Frodeman, R., Klein, J. T., & Pacheco, R. C. D. S. (Eds.). (2017*). The Oxford handbook of interdisciplinarity*. Oxford University Press.

Greenberger, S. W. (2020). Creating a guide for reflective practice: applying Dewey's reflective thinking to document faculty scholarly engagement. *Reflective Practice, 21*(4), 458-472.

Grunefeld, H., Prins, F. J., van Tartwijk, J., & Wubbels, T. (2022). Development of educational leaders' adaptive expertise in a professional development programme. *International Journal for Academic Development, 27*(1), 58-70.

Hartman, H. J. (1998). Metacognition in teaching and learning: An introduction. *Instructional Science*, 1-3.

Haynes, C., & Leonard, J. B. (2010). From surprise parties to mapmaking: Undergraduate journeys toward interdisciplinary understanding. *The Journal of Higher Education, 81*(5), 645-666.

Hendren, C. O., & Ku, S. T. H. (2019). The Interdisciplinary Executive Scientist: connecting scientific ideas, resources and people. In *Strategies for Team Science Success* (pp. 363-373). Springer.

Huysmans, M. (2023). The Market for Kidneys: Bridging Introductory Courses in Economics and Ethics. *Journal of Interdisciplinary Studies in Education.*

Ibarra, H., & Barbulescu, R. (2010). Identity as narrative: Prevalence, effectiveness, and consequences of narrative identity work in macro work role transitions. *Academy of management review, 35*(1), 135-154.

Kalis, A. (2023). How Concepts Travel In Actual Spaces: The Interdisciplinary Classroom As A Behavior Setting. *Journal of Interdisciplinary Studies in Education.*

Klein, J. T. (1996). *Crossing boundaries: Knowledge, disciplinarities, and interdisciplinarities.* University of Virginia Press.

Kurtti, E. (2022). *Making sense of cross-disciplinarity in university leaders' talk.*

Lin, X., Schwartz, D. L., & Hatano, G. (2018). Toward teachers' adaptive metacognition. In *Educational psychologist* (pp. 245-255). Routledge.

Lindvig, K. (2017). *Creating interdisciplinarity within monodisciplinary structures* (Doctoral dissertation, University of Copenhagen, Faculty of Science, Department of Science Education).

Lindvig, K., & Ulriksen, L. (2019). Different, difficult, and local: A review of interdisciplinary teaching activities. *The Review of Higher Education, 43*(2), 697-725.

Lutz, C. (2022). Recognition and promotion of faculty work: Practices emerging at the intersection between faculty development and educational renewal. *New Directions for Higher Education, 2021*(193-194), 37-44.

Lutz, C., Bouwens, A., & Van Goch, M. (in press). College classroom diversity as a source of scholarly learning for teachers. *College Teaching*.

Lutz, C., Untaru, L., & Van Goch, M. (2021). Developing a shared syllabus template as a living document of inclusive practices in a teaching and learning community. In *Proceedings of the 7th International Conference on Higher Education Advances* (pp. 481-489).

Lutz, C., Van Goch, M., & Baker, V. (2021, August 23-27). *Shape your own professional future through guided reflection exercises* [Conference presentation]. European Association for Research into Learning and Instruction, Gothenburg.

Lyall, C. (2019). *Being an interdisciplinary academic: How institutions shape university careers*. Springer.

Mansilla, V. B. (2005). Assessing student work at disciplinary crossroads. *Change: The Magazine of Higher Learning, 37*(1), 14–21.

Markauskaite, L., & Goodyear, P. (2017). Epistemic fluency and professional education. *Innovation, Knowledgeable Action and Actionable Knowledge*.

Meijer, P. C. (2011). The role of crisis in the development of student teachers' professional identity. In *Navigating in educational contexts* (pp. 41-54). SensePublishers, Rotterdam.

Neumann, A. (2009). *Professing to learn: Creating tenured lives and careers in the American research university*. JHU Press.

Newell, W. H. (2009). *Interdisciplinarity in undergraduate general education*. In R. Frodeman, J. T. Klein & C. Mitcham (Eds.), The Oxford handbook on interdisciplinarity. Oxford: Oxford University Press.

Repko, A. F., & Szostak, R. (2017). *Interdisciplinary research: Process and theory*. Sage Publications.

Rodgers, C. R. (2002). Seeing student learning: Teacher change and the role of reflection. *Harvard Educational Review, 72*(2), 230.

Schön, D. A. (1983). *The reflective practitioner: How professionals think in action*. New York: Basic Books.

Spelt, E. J., Biemans, H. J., Tobi, H., Luning, P. A., & Mulder, M. (2009). Teaching and learning in interdisciplinary higher education: A systematic review. *Educational Psychology Review, 21*(4), 365-378.

Thomson, K. E., & Trigwell, K. R. (2018). The role of informal conversations in developing university teaching? *Studies in Higher Education, 43*(9), 1536-1547.

Van Goch, M. (in press). Naar een raamwerk voor het identificeren, classificeren en inventariseren van interdisciplinair onderwijs. *Tijdschrift voor Hoger Onderwijs*.

Vink, C., de Greef, L., Post, G., & Wenting, L. (2017). *Designing interdisciplinary education: A practical handbook for university teachers*. Amsterdam University Press.

Weinert, F. (1987). *Introduction and Overview: Metacognition and motivation as determinants of effective learning and understanding*. In F. Weinert & R. Kluwe, eds., Metacognition, Motivation and Understanding. Hillsdale, NJ: Lawrence Erlbaum Associates.

MEREL VAN GOCH, PhD, is an Assistant Professor at the interdisciplinary Liberal Arts and Sciences undergraduate program at Utrecht University, The Netherlands. Her research and teaching are both motivated by the goal of providing people with the optimal circumstances to explore and foster their talents and interests. She is interested in how and what students and scholars learn, especially in interdisciplinary contexts. Her research includes metacognition, creativity, and other competences relevant to higher education, and her teaching methods emphasize students' self-directed learning. Email: m.m.vangoch@uu.nl

CHRISTEL LUTZ, PhD, is Associate Professor of Psychology and Director of Education at Liberal Arts and Sciences College University College Utrecht, and Principal Fellow at the Centre for Academic Teaching and Learning, both at Utrecht University, the Netherlands. She teaches on learning and motivation, and as a scholar she is interested in what makes learning communities thrive, for example in student-teacher partnership. She does practice-based research in the field of faculty development. Email: c.i.lutz@uu.nl

Manuscript submitted: ***October 20, 2022***
Manuscript revised: ***November 27, 2022***
Accepted for publication: ***January 14, 2023***

Book Review

The Impoverishment of the American College Student

Koch, J. V. (2019). *The impoverishment of the American college student*. The Brookings Institution. pp. 271. ISBN: 978-0815732617.

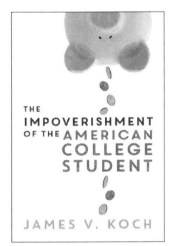

Higher education has long held a significant place in the national discourse and collective consciousness on social mobility (Roth, 2019). The cost of higher education in the United States, however, seems to conflict with this narrative. While a degree may offer opportunities, the price tag needs to be called into question. Some people have worked to shine a light on this problem, though. There has been a noteworthy emphasis placed on the debt amassed by individuals and their families to finance higher education. The total student loan debt currently sits at approximately $1.8 trillion. In *The Impoverishment of the American College Student*, economist James V. Koch attempts to unpack the complexities.

Koch offers several clear yet complex explanations for the staggering amount of student loan debt in the United States. First, federal and state governments have substantially decreased funding for higher education institutions. Second, higher education institutions have increased tuition and fees at a notable rate. Third, household incomes have remained consistently stagnant relative to inflation. While each of these economic functions may not be overly problematic when they occur individually, their nexus is altogether catastrophic for individuals and their families. Moreover, this problem is only made worse by the relative ease of acquiring student loans from the federal government. Koch notes, "Nearly 40 percent of all individuals between ages twenty and forty now have some student debt" (p. 51). Koch is quick to point out, however, that the majority of individuals and families are able to manage the student loan debt until the balance is resolved.

It is paramount to consider the individuals and families whose lives become deeply burdened by student loan debt, though. Koch suggests that student loan debt significantly impacts the behavior of those struggling to handle the payments. Examples of changes to behavior are decreases in home ownership, little or no retirement savings, and reductions in marriages rates (Valez et al., 2019). Of course, not all of these changes occur after completing a degree. Some students select a major based on projected income, and other students withdraw from the program of study to prevent further debt. Koch contends, "For some former students, their outstanding student debt burden has become the defining characteristic of their lives" (p. 63). It is clear that student loan debt often brings with it colossal stress for those individuals who want to expand their potential through the pursuit of higher education as well as for their families who serve to support them on their journeys. Despite the burden, many students see the loans as being worth it to obtain degrees (Nuckols et al., 2020).

The Impoverishment of the American College Student has strengths that warrant recognition. Despite the complicated nature of financial operations in higher education, Koch is able to address the mechanisms in a way that is digestible for both specialist and generalist readers. He makes a claim and supports his position through comprehensive deployments of data from multiple sources. This includes a variety of tables and charts that offer visual representations of data that serve as evidence. Koch is sure to clearly and concisely unpack any terminology that is needed to understand his argument. Even though the topic of his book is convoluted, Koch strives to ensure maximum comprehension for all readers in order to foster change surrounding the finance of higher education. In fact, he concludes with a suite of strategies that leaders might enact to move toward remedying the problem.

On the other hand, *this book* has some challenges that must also be addressed. One obvious challenge is that the title of the book does not align with the content of the book. As previously mentioned, the book focuses on shifts in higher education and society at large that push students and their families to take out exuberate amounts of loans to fund degrees. It is possible that a fraction of the students who obtain loans will experience impoverishment, but it is paramount to recognize that a small fraction of people actually experiences that. Another fundamental limitation is that the book is completely devoid of the human element. In other words, Koch relies purely on quantitative data to support these claims when qualitative data might have made the book that much stronger. Humanization through narratives, then, could help readers to see how people's daily lives are impacted.

This book is a recommended text for anyone hoping to gain insight on the current state of higher education finance in the United States. In particular, it provides a rich analysis of the mind-numbing quantity of student loan debt. Koch offers much more than a description and explanation of the situation, though. He is also critiquing the actors and actions that maintain an ecosystem in which this is made possible. He states, "Mainstream higher education organizations actively propagate such views, which are oft-repeated in higher education circles, because they largely excuse institutions from significant blame for most of the affordability and student debt problems that clearly do exist" (p. 213). This book, then, serves as a call to action for leaders in higher education to enact serious and sustainable organizational change to ensure that higher education is equitable for all.

References

Nuckols, W. L., Bullington, K. E., & Gregory, D. E. (2020). Was it worth it? Using student loans to finance a college degree. *Higher Education Politics & Economics, 6*, 1–19. https://doi.org/10.32674/hepe.v6i1.1358

Roth, G. (2019). *The educated underclass: Students and the false promise of social mobility*. Pluto Press.

Valez, E., Cominole, M., & Bentz, A. (2019). Debt burden after college: The effect of student loan debt on graduates' employment, additional schooling, family formation, and home ownership. *Education Economics, 27*(2), 186–206. https://doi.org/10.1080/09645292.2018.1541167

Bio

Jacob Kelley is a PhD student in the Department of Educational Foundations, Leadership, and Technology at Auburn University. He uses qualitative and quantitative methods to examine the complexities of adult learning in multiple contexts. In particular, he focuses on three constructs relevant to adult learning: effectiveness, engagement, and equity. His other interests are social change, international students, civic education, and program evaluation. His scholarship has been published in *New Directions for Teaching and Learning, Journal of Effective Teaching in Higher Education, Journal of Interdisciplinary Studies in Education*, and *Journal of Educational Thought*. He currently works in the Biggio Center for the Enhancement of Teaching and Learning at Auburn University. E-mail: jkk0019@auburn.edu

Printed in Germany
by Amazon Distribution
GmbH, Leipzig